# FORT SELDEN
## 1865–1891

The Birth, Life, and Death
of a Frontier Fort in New Mexico

# FORT SELDEN
## 1865–1891

### The Birth, Life, and Death
### of a Frontier Fort in New Mexico

A New Mexico Centennial History Series Book

## Allan J. Holmes

Illustrations by Katherine Frietze

SUNSTONE
PRESS

SANTA FE

Sunstone books may be purchased for educational, business, or sales promotional use. For information please write: Special Markets Department, Sunstone Press, P.O. Box 2321, Santa Fe, New Mexico 87504-2321.

Book and Cover design ▸ Vicki Ahl
Body typeface ▸ Franklin Gothic Book
Printed on acid free paper

Library of Congress Cataloging-in-Publication Data

Holmes, Allan J., 1936-
  Fort Selden, New Mexico, 1865-1891 : the birth, life, and death of a frontier fort in New Mexico / by Allan J. Holmes ; illustrations by Katherine Frietze.
     p. cm. -- (A New Mexico centennial history series book)
  Includes bibliographical references.
  ISBN 978-0-86534-737-3 (softcover : alk. paper)
 1.  Fort Selden (N.M.)--History. 2.  Fort Selden (N.M.)--Social life and customs. 3.  Frontier and pioneer life--New Mexico--Fort Selden. 4.  United States. Army--Military life--History--19th century. 5.  Soldiers--New Mexico--Fort Selden--History--19th century. 6.  Community life--New Mexico--Fort Selden--History--19th century. I. Title.
  F804.F65H65 2010
  978.9'66--dc22

                        2009046711

Published in

WWW.SUNSTONEPRESS.COM
SUNSTONE PRESS / POST OFFICE BOX 2321 / SANTA FE, NM 87504-2321 /USA
(505) 988-4418 / ORDERS ONLY (800) 243-5644 / FAX (505) 988-1025

# Dedication

This book is dedicated to Victoria, my chief critic and editor, to the Friends of Fort Selden, and to the staff at Fort Selden State Monument. Without their encouragement and support the manuscript and notes would have never become a book. I add a special thank you to my daughters, Kathy who did the illustrations and Ann-Marie whose computer expertise was highly appreciated.

# Contents

*Ruins of Fort Selden*

# Preface

Fort Selden was a frontier post built in the Territory of New Mexico in 1865 and occupied until 1891 by the United States Army in its battle against the general lawlessness of the region and the hostile Native Americans of southern New Mexico. It was named for Colonel Henry R. Selden, 1st New Mexico Infantry Regiment, who as a captain in the regular army fought in the Civil War battles of Valverde and Glorietta in New Mexico. He was promoted to brevet major in 1863, but resigned his regular commission and accepted the rank of colonel of volunteers in the 1st New Mexico Infantry. His first task was to recruit a regiment of New Mexican volunteers for General James H. Carleton, Commander of the Department of New Mexico. After the regiment was organized in 1864, he was given command of Fort Union, where he died 2 February 1865. Carleton, then in his memory, designated the new fort to be built near Las Cruces as Fort Selden.

As a young boy when I wandered through the decaying walls of Fort Selden, hiding behind them to shoot at imaginary cattle rustlers, horse thieves, and raiders, the excitement was almost too much to bear. Envisioning the troopers leaving the post through the sally port at a gallop with their flags flying was a glorious exercise, and made real by the Saturday afternoon westerns and cavalry movies of the 1940s and 1950s. Yet, after serving the United States Army for almost 30 years in posts across the United States and other parts of the world, I can now see how dreary, monotonous, and boring the daily life must have been for the soldiers stationed at Fort Selden. My research into their daily routines has deepened the respect I hold for these men and their efforts to protect the southern part of New Mexico.

A simple epitaph for Fort Selden would read, "It was built, accomplished its mission, and was abandoned." But this fails to show the tremendous impact that the fort had on the surrounding area. Two Fort Selden researchers, Timothy Cohrs and Hugh M. Milton, have concentrated on the commanders, units, battles, and patrols of the men of the fort and for the most part have ignored its effects on and relationships with the local communities. Whereas historians Robert Frazer, Francis Prucha, Darlis Miller, and others have shown that the United States Army through its building and supplying the small forts of the frontier contributed greatly to the economic growth and development of communities in the vicinity of the forts. This, too, was the case of Fort Selden. Throughout the fort's history, not only did the post provide for local security, but it also contributed dramatically to the economic and social growth of the region.

Detachments of the 1st California Cavalry Regiment, the 1st New Mexico Volunteer Infantry Regiment, and the 1st California Veteran Infantry Regiment began constructing Fort Selden on 8 May 1865. Brevet Lieutenant Colonel Nelson H. Davis, the Inspector General of the Department of New Mexico, had selected and surveyed a site for the fort about eighteen miles north of Las Cruces. The post, similar to other small southwestern posts of the time, was designed to accommodate one troop of cavalry and one company of infantry. Throughout the post's early history (1865–1878), its complement was two companies, although for a time both companies were cavalry. Fort Selden was temporarily abandoned during Victorio's War (1878–1880) because of the requirement for troops in the field. Then in the 1880s the soldiers came back to Fort Selden, when the crews of the Atchison, Topeka, and Santa Fe (AT&SF) railroad, who were laying track south across the Jornada del Muerto, needed protection from raiders. The post was again occupied on 25 December 1880, but during the final phase of Fort Selden's history, 1881–1891, the normal contingent was only one company of infantry.

The post was constructed of adobe bricks and it required an immense amount of maintenance to keep it livable. There are conflicting reports on the overall appearance of the post. Lydia Spencer Lane, wife of the Post Commander in 1869, stated in her book, *I Married a Soldier*, "Our new station was a quiet rather unattractive place." In contrast to her rather denigrating comment, a Las Cruces newspaper, the *Borderer*, reported on 14 February 1872, "Fort Selden is considered one of the most pleasant military posts on the whole Southwestern frontier." Captain Arthur MacArthur, commander of the post from 1884 to 1886, stated in a report to his headquarters that the post was well situated and presented the best appearance of any that he had seen in New Mexico.

Fort Selden was established as a base camp; it was not a fighting fortress such as Fort Ticonderoga. It was essentially a base camp for the soldiers who were required to patrol or scout the region from the Florida Mountains on the west, to the Sacramento and Guadalupe mountains on the east, north to Cañada Alamosa, and south to the Mexican border (Figure 1). This was an area of approximately 15,000 square miles, an overwhelming amount of territory to cover with only a hundred or so men

The soldiers assigned to Fort Selden had many varied missions. They defended against hostile Native Americans; chased stock raiders; corralled outlaws; escorted the mail; protected travelers and wagon trains; and provided relief support to the local citizenry during floods and epidemics. As the Apache threat slowly dwindled and the railroad system developed to the point where troops could be centralized and moved quickly by rail to the place of need, the small, inefficient, and uneconomical forts of the Southwest were abandoned and the soldiers were gathered at regimental posts. Fort Selden was considered as one of the regimental headquarters, but not selected.

The competition for the regional regimental post of southern New Mexico and west Texas was intense and close. President Chester A. Arthur had asked Congress on 3 March 1882, for funds to increase Fort Selden to a regimental post of twelve companies. However, the Commander of the Army, General William T. Sherman, after completing his reconnaissance of the area in the spring of 1882, was convinced that Fort Bliss near the town of El Paso, Texas was a better suited due to the number of railroads serving El Paso, so Fort Selden lost its most important battle. The last detachment of the 24th Infantry Regiment departed Fort Selden in January 1891, and the post was left to the eroding effects of time and weather.

The Department of the Interior had considered establishing an Indian school at Fort Selden. However, this idea faded and the land reverted to public domain. The land then passed through several owners, and the last was Harry H. Bailey who obtained the land in 1944. On his death in 1962 his son gave the land to the state, and now the State Monuments Bureau of the Museum of New Mexico is preserving the ruins.

For many years Fort Selden's ruins have been one of the historic attractions of the Mesilla Valley of southern New Mexico. Sign posts along I-25 and state road 185, tourist guidebooks, and the local people proudly point the way to the remains of the fort. Several times a year the Friends of Fort Selden and other re-enactment companies hold enactment camps at the fort, proud to show how life in a frontier may have been. The staff at the fort has a historic and cultural center near the ruins where artifacts from Fort Selden unearthed by several archeological digs by New Mexico State University are displayed. A film can be seen as you begin your tour of the fort.

Darlis Miller and I were asked to share our knowledge of the life and times of a frontier fort in the making of that film. Rather Darlis was asked and she dragged me along as she was my advisor on my master's thesis, entitled Fort Selden. This book is the larger story of the fort and an expansion of that thesis. I hope that in some way this book contributes to the understanding of the hardships suffered by and the successes of the soldiers who served at the fort, and the impact that this fort had on the economic and social development of southern New Mexico.

For ease of reading I have left off the word regiment in most cases. When you see the numbered infantry or cavalry unit, the word regiment is implied, 13th Infantry, should be read as 13th Infantry Regiment. I also recognize that the U.S. Army did not begin calling the cavalry company a troop until 1883, but in order not to confuse the reader by switching in mid stream, I have referred to the infantry unit as a company and the cavalry unit as a troop throughout the book.

—Allan J. Holmes

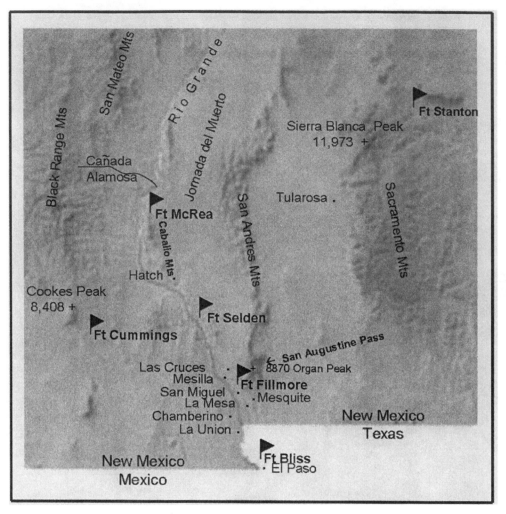

*Figure 1: Fort Selden's Area of Operations*

Distances:

Fort Selden to Fort Marcy (Santa Fe)

250 miles

Fort Selden to Fort Stanton

150 miles

Fort Selden to Arizona

120 miles

*Colonel Henry R. Selden*

# 1

# Birth of a Fort

## Necessity

The American Civil War began quite early for the residents of the Mesilla Valley and southern New Mexico. The Confederates under the command of Colonel John R. Baylor had occupied La Mesilla in 1861 with very little resistance. Fort Fillmore, located south of La Mesilla, had provided protection to the area from Native Americans, but according to the post surgeon, Major James C. McKee, was abandoned quite ignobly to Baylor's forces after destroying the military stores.[1] Major Isaac Lynde, the Union Commander of Fillmore, attempted to get his command to Fort Stanton in the Sacramento Mountains, but was caught and defeated on the west side of the Organ Mountains about sixteen miles east of Las Cruces partially due to his men filling their canteens with medicinal alcohol in lieu of water. This action and the following Confederate invasion both north and west denuded the Mesilla Valley of military defenses and was a signal to the Apaches to increase their raids on the settlers of the valley. Moreover, the Confederate operations did not stop at the town of La Mesilla.

General Henry H. Sibley, who had recently given up command of Fort Union in northern New Mexico Territory, resigned his United States Army commission and joined the Confederate cause. He convinced

President Jefferson Davis that possession of New Mexico Territory was crucial in establishing a route to the California ports and gold. After capturing La Mesilla and designating it the capital of the newly established Confederate territory, Sibley sent forces west to Tucson while he drove up the Rio Grande, defeating the Union forces at Valverde (February 1862) and occupying Albuquerque and Santa Fe. He then moved to capture the military stores at Fort Union, but was forced into a retreat south to El Paso and finally to San Antonio, when his supply wagons were burned at Glorieta in March 1862. The Confederate invasion of New Mexico Territory destroyed crops, wreaked havoc on the economic base, and provided the Apaches with a renewed resolution to drive the settlers out of the territory. William F. Arny, secretary of the territory, reported in the Santa Fe *New Mexican*:

> The destruction caused by the Texan invasion in 1861 and 1862 has had a most disastrous effect on the country. The Indians seeing that the whites were at war increased in boldness and compelled the abandonment of many mines and settlements.[2]

The invasion also brought into New Mexico a strong-willed and controversial man who was to guide the territory's military efforts for the next five years. James Henry Carleton was a career soldier who had seen duty in the Aroostuck and Mexican wars, and had been stationed as a captain at Fort Union. He knew the territory and the local inhabitants well. He had been brevetted a major for gallantry and meritorious service at the battle of Buena Vista in 1847, but gave up that rank in the summer of 1862 when he joined the 1st Volunteer California Regiment as a colonel. It was this force that came to the rescue of New Mexico.

Colonel Carleton marched his 2,000-man California Column across the southern desert, recaptured Tucson in June 1862, and reached the Mesilla Valley by August 1862.[3] He was promoted to brigadier general during the march to New Mexico, and on arrival in New Mexico replaced General E.R.S. Canby, the Union commander at the battle of Valverde. Carleton was then appointed as the Commander of the Department of

New Mexico in September 1862 with the rank of major general, and established his headquarters at Fort Marcy in Santa Fe. His department included southern Colorado, Arizona, parts of west Texas, and all of present-day New Mexico.

In his own words he was a man of little patience for those who had taken the oath to the Confederacy, drank while on duty, became impaired from drink, or were dishonest. He was especially hard on what he referred to as "unprincipled officers."[4]

The protection for the Mesilla Valley was now to come from a combined force of the California and New Mexican Volunteers and remnants of the 5th Infantry. General Carleton was faced with two separate missions. First he had to defend the region from more possible Confederate invasions, this was done well, but secondly he had to provide protection to the residents from hostile Native Americans. This protection was rather ineffective at first. Carleton wrote that "the Indians aware that our efforts could not for the time be turned to them commenced robbing the inhabitants of their stock and killed a great number of people."[5] It was this second mission that eventually led to the building of Fort Selden.

General Carleton established a subordinate command for southern New Mexico and Arizona under Colonel, later Brigadier General, Joseph R. West. West's headquarters was established first at La Mesilla, New Mexico Territory, then moved to Hart's Mill (present day El Paso, Texas), and finally moved to Prescott, Arizona. West was charged with the defense of the southern area until 1866 when the District of Texas was created.

West did well against the Confederate threat. Colonel John Baylor, CSA, who had been successful in 1861 against La Mesilla and Fort Fillmore, later raised a large force in San Antonio, but rumors of his approach toward New Mexico ended when he was sent east. Carleton was still certain that Baylor would turn toward El Paso and urged his commanders to be vigilant. He wrote, "Baylor's force of 6000 men shipped from San Antonio to coast, but will doubtless soon come in this direction."[6]

Carleton's worries about Baylor proved groundless, but another confederate raider, Skillman, did move in Carleton's direction. West sent a patrol from El Paso toward Fort Quitman (about 70 miles south of El Paso), which intercepted and destroyed Skillman's small raiding force. However successful the Union forces were in skirmishes with the Texans, the same success was not gained against the hostile Native Americans.

Carleton planned to make efficient use of his minimal forces by subduing the New Mexico tribes one at a time. He outlined this plan in a letter to the Adjutant General of the Army, Brigadier General Lorenzo Thomas, on 1 February 1863, stating, "It is not practical with my present force and amount of means to make effective demonstrations on more than one tribe at a time."[7] First he sent Colonel Christopher (Kit) Carson and the 1st New Mexico Volunteer Infantry to reoccupy Fort Stanton, build Fort Sumner, and subdue the Mescalero Apaches. Then in the second phase, he sent forces from El Paso and La Mesilla to pacify the Mimbres Apaches. The plan included building a new post, Fort West, to support operations in the Gila region. Fort West (after Carleton's departure in late 1866, it was renamed Fort Bayard for General G. D. Bayard who was killed at the battle of Fredericksburg), was located about five miles northwest of the mining community of Santa Rita del Cobre. It was started in 1863 using the vigas, frames, and lumber from the abandoned Fort Fillmore, and served to protect the rich mining area from the Mimbres Apache. The presence of the fort merely served to move the Apache elsewhere, but to Carleton it was a very successful venture. He reported to the War Department on 1 February 1863 that, "the Mescaleros are completely subdued . . . and expeditions into the Gila have been quite successful. . . . I now propose to punish the Navaho (sic)."[8] One must admire Carleton's optimism for his solution was very similar to using your fingers in a dike when there are more than ten holes: when one is covered it ceases to be a problem but when you remove your finger to cover another hole, water again begins to flow.

As soon as Carleton drew forces from the southern forts to fight the Navajos, the Apaches renewed their raids on the settlements and ranches in the vacated area. This did not sit well with those suffering through the raids in the southern part of the state. Ugly comments toward Carleton and the army surfaced after Native Americans had raided the towns of La Mesa, Chamberino, Las Cruces, and Doña Ana.

A letter to the editor of the Santa Fe *New Mexican* complained, "on Monday last, Indians entered the town of Las Cruces, a military post, and took stock from the corral of Alban Duran . . . the Army did not respond."[9] Again on 17 February in a letter to the *New Mexican*, the citizens showed their displeasure by stating that Carleton was too busy with "his plan" to deal with the robberies and murders of the people. Another writer lamented the conditions, "It is unsafe to move outside the settlements of New Mexico without strong military protection."[10]

Carleton did have his supporters. An article in the Santa Fe *New Mexican*, 5 December 1863, reported:

> The most efficient means ever exerted to subjugate the Indian in this country are those now being carried on by General Carleton. No officer remains idle at the post or in places of no military influence. He is establishing new posts at the most important points and is sending troops into the heart of Indian country.

Despite the hyperbole, the need for a military post in the lower Rio Grande region was obvious, and General Carleton had promised Colonel West and the people of the Mesilla Valley that a fort would be built in the vicinity of Las Cruces or La Mesilla as soon as soldiers were available.[11] However, the post would have to wait until Carleton had the Navajos on a reservation. This occurred in late 1864 when Carson defeated the Navajos with a "scorched earth" strategy at Canyon de Chelly and marched them (known to the Navajo people as the Long Walk) across New Mexico to Carleton's new reservation at Bosque Redondo located near Fort Sumner on the Pecos River in eastern New Mexico. Now Carleton had the units and soldiers available for a post in the Mesilla Valley, and he turned his attention back to the problem of Native American raids in the south.

## Location

A short notice in the Santa Fe *New Mexican*, 14 November 1863, brought onto the stage the next important player in the establishment of Fort Selden, "Brevet Lieutenant Colonel Nelson H. Davis arrived in New Mexico last week. He is to be the Inspector General. . . . He has the appearance of being an officer with the right truck in him." As the Inspector General for the command, Davis had the responsibility to inspect the posts, troops, equipment, and to insure the highest morale, welfare, and general efficiency possible in the Military Department of New Mexico's outlying posts. General Carleton added to these tasks, the job of selecting sites for the new forts being considered by the command.

Davis was a career officer. He was a graduate of West Point and a veteran of both the Mexican and the Civil wars. He was brevetted a first lieutenant for gallantry and meritorious conduct at the battles of Contreras and Churubusco during the Mexican War. He was later brevetted a lieutenant colonel for gallantry and meritorious service at the battle of Gettysburg, but reverted to major when he joined the Department of New Mexico.[12] Davis had reported in on 6 November as a major, but Carleton wanted him as the Department Inspector General which required a higher rank, so re-promoted him and told Washington about it in a message sent 22 November 1863. Then in 1864 Carleton recommended him again to the War Department for promotion to brevet colonel for gallantry in action against the Apache in Arizona Territory while selecting the site for Fort Goodwin.[13] He retired from the service in 1885 as a brigadier general and died in May, 1890.

Davis during his routine inspection tour of the various forts and camps in the southern portion of the command in early 1865 conducted a reconnaissance to select a site for Fort Selden near Las Cruces. In a message to Carleton on 8 April 1865, Davis did not reflect on the scenic beauty or the solitude of the site, but simply and clinically described its physical aspects. "The locality I have selected is on a mesa flat, being on a point of land projecting southwest toward a bend in the Rio Grande."[14]

Today, standing in the center of the parade field of the ruins of the old fort and looking at the surrounding terrain it is easy to understand why Davis selected this particular site. It is located on a small ridge of high ground, or bluff, about one-half mile east of the Rio Grande with mountains on both the east and west. The small bluff, or mesa, provides a panoramic view of the Mesilla Valley to the south and the Franklin Mountains near El Paso. The Robledo Mountains, across the river to the west, overshadow the post, and with the Doña Ana Mountains on the east, form a narrow passageway from the Jornada del Muerto into the Mesilla Valley.

The Jornada del Muerto is an eighty-five mile stretch of gently rolling basin, which runs north and south between the Caballo Mountains on the west and the San Andres Mountains on the east. Because of the lack of arroyos and cuts that characterize the Rio Grande's bed and the eastern slope of the Black Range, this basin had been the primary wagon route (called the Camino Real and later the Post Road) for settlers since the early Spanish explorers. Now Interstate 25 no longer follows the Jornada del Muerto route because with the advent of the automobile, the cuts and arroyos that hindered horse or cattle drawn wagons are no longer a problem. It does follow the trail for a short distance north of Radium Springs before dropping back down on the western slopes of the Caballo Mountains, but the Burlington Northern and Santa Fe railroad still follows the old trail from Valverde to Fort Selden.

Though the Jornada provided an easy route for the wagons, the route for people and animals was not quite as delightful. As the wagon route left the ford of the Rio Grande at Fort Selden just north of the post, it climbed further up the bluff to gain the basin and left water behind. The critical element to the movement of people and animals in the Southwest was, of course, water, and water was in scant supply on the Jornada. Without water many travelers died, hence the name Jornada del Muerto, or journey of death.[15] During the late 1860s after Fort Selden was built, John Martin, a businessman from Las Cruces, dug a deep well with the help of the army at Aleman's station about halfway up the Jornada. This well provided welcome relief to Fort Selden's patrols, travelers crossing the Jornada, and later became a water stop for the

Acheson, Topeka, and Santa Fe railroad (now the Burlington Northern and Santa Fe).

Davis insured a steady, if somewhat muddy, supply of water for Fort Selden by establishing the reservation near the river. He also insured relief from the bugs, fevers, and chills associated with the wetlands by locating the post up on the small mesa. However, it was located close enough to the wetlands and bosque (woods) of the river to insure building materials. Colonel Davis had received a special request from General Carleton to insure an adequate supply of "cottonwoods [trees] for vigas."[16]

The Post Surgeon reported in his annual report in 1870 that Davis had accomplished this tough task.

> The reservation is four miles square. The soil is sandy and sterile, resting on volcanic rocks. The ground rises gradually to the north for about four miles; on the south it slopes to the river bottom. The cottonwoods grow along the river, a coarse and scanty growth of grass on the reservation, with plenty of cacti and stunted mesquite comprise the botany of the vicinity. Deer, antelope, and bear are found in the mountains. Wolves and skunks are annoyingly numerous about the post. At the river, beavers are plenty.[17]

The current staff at the monument reports that though the wolves are gone, the skunks are still annoyingly numerous.

The specific military reasons for choosing the site for Fort Selden are easily established. The site afforded an adequate water supply, it was situated on high ground, and it provided good observation of the area especially when a observation post was established on Lookout peak in the Robledo Mountains. Also a main consideration was that the site had easy access to the area's roads. Fort Selden was located on the only north-south transportation route, and later Carleton made the fort an east-west terminal as well by building a road to the west to connect to Fort Cummings and beyond. He wrote to The Adjutant General, Brigadier General Lorenzo Thomas on 14 August 1865:

Fort Selden is located on the left bank of the Rio Grande where the Jornada [Del Muerto] first strikes the river. It is an important point for the protection of travelers as well as to protect the flocks and herds of the people living along the Rio Grande in what is called the Mesilla Valley. A ferry and a new road will be opened to Goodnight Station on the main stage route of the old Overland Line from Mesilla to California.[18]

The ruts of this trail heading west from Fort Selden can still be seen in some places, but Carleton misstated the station. The trail led to the Good Sight station at the base of Good Sight Peak. Its ruins are now on the Hyatt ranch. He must have confused this station with the old cattle trail in eastern New Mexico called the Goodnight Trail. He did correct himself in a subsequent message to the Adjutant General in September 1865.

Another important military consideration was the distance that a cavalry or mounted infantry unit could move in a day. The army's standard distance for a day's ride for mounted troops was twenty-five miles, but under forced march conditions a unit could cover fifty miles. Since the southwest posts were small and short of manpower, units from various posts would be combined in order to conduct large field operations called "converging columns." To facilitate this merging of forces, Carleton built his forts approximately fifty miles apart. This allowed for cooperation between the forts, and reinforcements for a unit in trouble were usually only a hard day's ride away.

A less obvious reason for selecting such a remote site (a day's ride from Las Cruces and La Mesilla) comes from Carleton's message to Davis on 1 September 1865. "The Forts of McRea, West, Cummings, and Selden attest to my views of getting the soldiers out of towns and away from alcohol and debauchery."[19] This attempt to get the soldiers away from the evils of civilization was not too successful for even as Fort Selden was being built, the town of Leasburg (referred to by the many commanders as a "hog ranch") sprang up within Davis' surveyed reservation.

Adolphe Lea, a merchant from Las Cruces and always referred to as an honorable gentleman by the commanders of Fort Selden, had established and filed a homestead claim at the same time that Davis was surveying the reservation. Lea claimed a portion of the fort's land and had built a small town on the disputed land. Commanders from 1866 to 1870 called for a survey and tried to evict Lea, but the town remained with its saloons, gambling, and prostitutes. The dispute was finally settled in November 1870 when President U. S. Grant approved a new boundary excluding the town of Leasburg leaving the Fort Selden Military Reservation with fifteen square miles instead of the original sixteen.

## Construction

Once the decision was made on a location for Fort Selden, the questions were now oriented toward the availability of building materials and the type of construction. The Chief Quartermaster for the Department of New Mexico, Colonel John McFerran, was interested in constructing the post as cheaply as possible. He requested that Davis "scout diligently" for trees or poles that could be used to form a framework. This method of construction was referred to in the Southwest as the "jacal" style. It required upright poles to form the walls, which were then chinked with mud to make them solid.

But Davis could not find sufficient trees in the area and to haul them from the Black Range or the Sacramento Mountains would be cost prohibitive. John Lemon, a businessman from La Mesilla, former member of the California Volunteers, and prominent politician, offered to build the fort for the army for the sum of $29,000, but General Carleton thought it could be built for a less than $20,000 with troop labor. Carleton's final decision was that the army would build the post with troop labor and use locally made adobes, sun dried bricks of mud and straw.

Carleton directed Captain James E. Whitlock, commanding the quartermaster depot and troops in Las Cruces, to begin construction of

Fort Selden in April 1865.

> By this mail you receive an order to establish Fort Selden. Turn over your post to Lieutenant Jennings. . . . You are authorized to take Lieutenant Oliphant, his First Sergeant, company records, two other sergeants, two corporals, and twenty of the most dissipated of his men.[20]

But Carleton did not want the soldiers building the fort to forget the primary mission of providing security to the area. In the same letter to Whitlock he stated, "You will need some mounted men, the best horses will be taken and kept in good condition for field service."

The plan (Figure 2) for constructing the post was simple and compact. Most of the buildings would be built around the parade field with the long axis of the field running north and south. Typical of most of the southwestern forts, it was envisioned as a cantonment area and patrol base, not a fighting fort.

The combined detachment of California and New Mexico volunteers arrived at the site on 8 May 1865 to begin building. The job facing these soldiers was not an easy one. It was the beginning of the summer heat of southern New Mexico, where temperatures above 100 degrees are fairly common. The small mesa Davis selected was covered with mesquite, creosote, yucca, rabbit bush, and many varieties of cactus. Each of these desert plants had a deep and stubborn root system. Their removal would cause men with modern machinery to put forth considerable effort, but these soldiers labored with only hand tools and draft animals.

The accomplishments of land clearing and construction in that environment probably should have been admired, but Carleton was less than pleased on his inspection tour in late May. He wrote to Whitlock, while at Fort Selden:

> You must get your store houses and hospital up at the earliest practical day. . . . Your officers are commissioned and paid to

direct the labors of your men . . . You will direct your officers to be at their place of duty . . . establish well organized fatigue parties each under an officer until such time that you have run out of officers. Then and only then use sergeants. . . . Commanders will turn out with their parties at fatigue call.[21]

The Las Cruces quartermaster officer, Captain Rufus Vose, also received a fair share of the blame for the slow building progress of the fort. There were insufficient tools such as shovels, hoes, and saws for the soldiers to do their work efficiently, and the quartermaster was spending a lot of time in Las Cruces with his "records." Carleton wrote to the chief quartermaster, "I wish to stir up the quartermaster down in this country. . . . They seem to be listless and lack or do not manifest zeal, energy, or snap."[22] After complaining about the leadership shown at the fort, Carleton provided an incentive to the troops. Those who were actually on the job and working were to be provided a gill (four fluid ounces) of whiskey per diem. In comparison a modern jigger or shot of whiskey is about 1.5 ounces so those at work got two shots plus an ounce. It seems hard liquor was fine if you were drinking it for the government and not to excess in the saloons of the hog ranch of Leasburg.

It is not clear who made the adobes used in the construction of the fort, but the assumption is that some expertise of the locals was needed. Carleton had used civilian contract labor to help make adobes at Forts McRea and Cummings and to rebuild Fort Craig, but there is no mention in the early reports that local laborers helped at Fort Selden. One local writer's complaint on 29 December 1865 in the Santa Fe *New Mexican* indicated that the soldiers did all of the construction work. The writer was quite perturbed that the troops were used in this manner: "The troops had been all summer engaged in the very military exercise of making adobes. . . . It is a shame that soldiers should be required to do such work."

The adobes were put together with mud mortar to form the eight-foot high walls. The windows and doorways were framed with lumber brought from Blazer's sawmill at Tularosa, New Mexico, a small community at the base of the Sacramento Mountains about 100 miles east of the fort. The walls were then covered with a flat roof. The roof was supported with rafters, locally called vigas, six to eight inch in diameter logs, spaced about two feet apart, running from the front wall to the back wall. These vigas were then covered with tule or cattails reeds and willow branches from the river, and plastered with mud. Needless to say, there were many complaints about leaky roofs and the rapid deterioration of the adobe from the summer thunderstorms and the winter rains.

The work on the fort progressed at a slow rate. Originally Carleton had planned to have the buildings erected by January 1866. However, in June 1866, Lieutenant Colonel Edward B. Willis, 1st New Mexico Volunteers, now commanding the post, reported that good progress was being made and estimated post would be finished in three months.[23] Yet, Lydia Spencer Lane, wife of the commander in 1869, remarked on her arrival in March, "The officers' quarters were not yet completed, but as the summer went by, the rooms in the house were finished one by one."[24] The post was essentially completed by 1870 though several of the buildings, one being the hospital, still did not have wood floors.[25] In February 1872, the editor of the *Borderer* visited Fort Selden as the guest of the commander and wrote a glowing report on the post: "Fort Selden is considered one of the most pleasant military posts on the whole Southwestern frontier."

The "most pleasant military post" was simply designed. The officers' row was built to the north of the parade field, while the two troop barracks and accompanying kitchens were on the south edge. The kitchens had root cellars dug just to the south. The hospital faced the parade field from the west and the administration building was on the east so that the parade field and its flag pole were the center of the post. Both the officers' row and the hospital had brush-roofed porches that Mrs. Lane noted were only a home for tarantulas and other desert bugs. Others also complained about the bugs and tarantulas dropping down from the roofs, but these brush covers remained for the shade until 1876. The surgeon in his monthly report dated 31 October 1876 reported that finally these "old bug infested shadings . . . were taken down and carted off."

The administration building had the only two-story portion of the fort, the post's courtroom that sat above the sally port. The court room was highly utilized as it also served as the District of New Mexico's court room for the southern area. It was here that the soldiers from Fort Cummings, Company A, 38th Infantry Regiment, who had mutinied were tried and convicted by a district court-martial board.

The corrals, east of the administration building, were also built of adobe with brush shade shelters for the animals. The bakery was on the far west side of the post and was equipped with outside mud ovens or hornos. The post cemetery not shown on the schematic is believed to be located to the northwest of the parade field. The post trader, or sutler's store, was located to the north of the officers' quarters on the post road facing east. There were no walls or redoubts enclosing the fort, so open to the desert, Fort Selden must have been a terrible place during the sand storms that darkened the skies from the New Mexican spring winds.

During the inactive phase of the post from 1878–1880 the walls and roofs deteriorated badly from the effects of the weather and the salvage operations to support other active forts. Upon reactivation in 1881, the only building fit for habitation was the post trader's building. In the subsequent reconstruction only sufficient quarters for one company were rebuilt, and the second story over the sally port was razed. Captain Arthur MacArthur, 13th Infantry, arriving in 1884, was aggressive and energetic in rebuilding and refurnishing the post. He obtained the flagpole from Fort Cummings, which was now closed, and furniture (such as wardrobes, sideboards, tables, and desks), from Fort McRea, also closed.[26] He detailed soldiers to work as masons, hounded headquarters for building funds and materials, and submitted detailed plans for the improvement of the barracks, storerooms, hospital, and quarters.

Construction and renovations at Fort Selden continued intermittently throughout the life of the post, from 1865 to 1891. Each commander revised, rebuilt, improved, and put his personality into the drab adobe walls of the fort. Blazer's sawmill at Tularosa furnished most of the lumber, and the citizens of the local communities provided the artisans, such as masons, carpenters, and plasterers, for these projects when the post had the money to pay them. As late as November 1889, innovative improvements, such as a bath house at the hot springs north of the post, were being added to make the soldier's life a little easier.[27] But even with all the efforts to build and create a livable environment from the harsh desert, the soldiers stationed at Fort Selden faced a truly boring and monotonous task with little relief.

*The Administration building circa 1876, courtesy Palace of the Governors Photo Archives (NMHM/DCA) 055040*

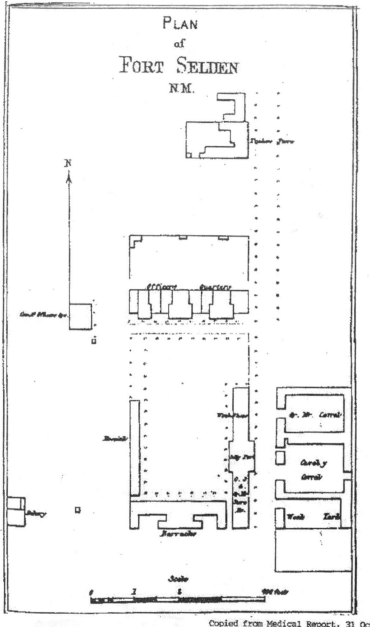

PLAN
of
FORT SELDEN
N.M.

Copied from Medical Report, 31 Oct 1876,
Fort Selden, RG 94, National Archives.

*Figure 2, Plan of Fort Selden*

*Statue honoring the troopers of the 9th Cavalry at Fort Selden*

# 2

# Life at the Fort

## Manpower

The troop units, officers, and non-commissioned officers who served at Fort Selden from 1865 to 1891 faced the same problems with manpower that confronted the entire regular army: too many missions, too few troops, too much alcohol, and too little pay. The demobilization of the massive Union army that had fought the Civil War began immediately after the surrender at Appomattox in 1865. More than one million men were released in a year's time, reducing the size of the army to 54,000 by 1866. All the volunteer units were mustered out, leaving a mere skeleton of an army charged with the responsibility of maintaining peace in the territory west of the Mississippi.[1] This small band of professionals was ultimately successful, but the issue was in doubt for many years.

Historian Robert M. Utley stated that, "by the end of 1866 the Regular Army authorized by the Act of July 28 . . . had been posted to the west to relieve the volunteers."[2] So it was with Fort Selden. The volunteer units under General Carleton, the 1st California Veteran Infantry, 1st California Cavalry, and the 1st New Mexico Volunteers (both infantry and cavalry) that had manned Fort Selden from May 1865 to August 1866 were mustered out in late 1866. Many of these officers and men from the California regiments remained in the area and became important members of the local communities.

As these volunteer units were dissolved, the 125th Infantry Regiment, a volunteer black unit that had been formed too late for action in the Civil War, and Troop K, 3rd Cavalry Regiment, assumed responsibility for the post.[3] The last volunteer unit of the 125th Infantry left Fort Selden in September 1867, and the companies of the 38th Infantry (Colored), a regular army black regiment commanded by white officers, and Troop K, 3rd Cavalry, were now providing for the security of the Mesilla Valley. These forces, the 3rd Cavalry and the 38th Infantry, ushered in a long line of regular army infantry and cavalry units both black and white that were the prime factors in the pacification efforts of the area.[4]

The units assigned to Fort Selden were rarely kept at the post for more than two years. Historian Don Rickey wrote:

> This rotation of units was a common practice among the regiments where it was feasible. . . It helped break the dull, monotonous routine. . . . The more fortunate ones soon discovered that the actual travel involved was the only real change, for life at one isolated post tended to be much like that at another.[5]

The rapid rotation may have relieved some of the boredom for the soldiers, but it created some problems. One serious problem was that the newly arriving commanders and soldiers knew neither the terrain nor the enemy. It probably took most of the rotation period for them to learn the area, and by the time the unit became familiar with the region, it moved on to a different post. Some might not have ever learned the area as evidenced by Captain Wilbur F. DuBois' message to Santa Fe in December 1870. When he and his company from the 15th Infantry were ordered to move from Fort Selden toward Arizona, he respectfully requested permission to hire a guide, as he did not know the water holes to the west.[6] Yet his area of operations extended west to the Florida Mountains almost to the Arizona territory, and he had been at Fort

Selden for over a year. In April 1874 Captain Chambers McKibben, 15th Infantry, reported to the Superintendent of Indian Affairs, that he was, "totally unacquainted with the tribes referred to, the country mentioned, and the people in the area." Captain Gregory Barrett, Company D, 10th Infantry, newly arrived in 1886, wrote the commander at Fort Bliss, who had asked about the condition of roads for wagon travel, ". . . river not fordable here, I understand that there is a crossing at [La] Mesilla."[7] However, there was not a crossing at La Mesilla as he learned later. In a subsequent message on 20 September Barrett reported to headquarters that the only crossing was by skiff, which was not much help for the Fort Bliss commander wanting to cross a wagon train.

Another Fort Selden commander answering a request for information about the geography and the Indians of the area in June 1884 replied to the effect that he and his unit had just arrived at Fort Selden and no one was sufficiently knowledgeable with the post to answer the questions.[8] Even the noted Captain Arthur MacArthur, 13th Infantry, commanding the post in 1886 indicated a lack of knowledge of his operational area. He had received a "be prepared to" mission from General Nelson A. Miles in Arizona during the chase of Geronimo's band in 1886. MacArthur had to request maps from the United States Land Office in Las Cruces for details about the area to the west of Fort Selden. He also asked the Land Office specifically for information about waterholes, ranches, streams, and trails in the Florida Mountains.[9] Yet, as with DuBois, the Floridas were part of his normal operating area.

The army policy of unit rotation also resulted in a large number of different companies and regiments serving at Fort Selden. The cavalry regiments included the 3rd, the 8th, and the 9th. The 9th Cavalry was a black unit that was nicknamed the Buffalo Soldiers by the Native Americans it fought against. The assigned regular army infantry units were the 38th, 10th, 13th, 15th, and the 24th. The 38th Infantry and the 24th Infantry were both black units. All of these units contributed to the growth and prosperity of the Mesilla Valley through their continuous efforts to keep peace in the valley and by the influx of money through their local purchases and payrolls.

## The Quantity and Quality of Soldiers

Low numbers of personnel assigned to the units continued to plague the commanders throughout the history of Fort Selden. The original force that began the post was a conglomerate of the remnants of units. The companies that had crossed the desert from California with General Carleton in 1862 had reached the end of their enlistment and most were not reenlisting. Colonel Selden's recruiting efforts for the new volunteer regiment solved the problem temporarily, but then the Civil War was over. Congress reduced army personnel ceilings from 54,000 to 37,313 by 1869, to 30,000 in 1870, and to 27,000 in 1874. This ceiling translated into an authorized manpower of 100 enlisted men for a cavalry troop and thirty-seven for an infantry company. Even with this low ceiling the army was never at full strength. Robert Utley noted, "Rarely . . . did the [Army of the West] rolls bear the names of more than 19,000 soldiers [it was authorized 25,000]."[10]

At Fort Selden the units were similarly affected. For example, Troop C, 8th Cavalry, assigned to Fort Selden from March 1871 to December 1874, had an average of fifty-seven assigned personnel in 1872 and averaged only forty-four men present for duty.[11] The infantry units were even smaller. Company B, 13th Infantry at Fort Selden in 1882, had an average of forty-one soldiers assigned with an average of only thirty-four men present for duty at any one time.[12] As would be expected the present-for-duty strength impacted heavily on the manpower available for patrol duty.

The strength for a particular patrol varied according to the number of men on sick call, post detail, in confinement, or absent without leave (AWOL). General William T. Sherman stated in 1873 that the number of men at a post "sick and on necessary detail about post equaled twenty-five per cent of the command."[13] These figures alone provide an indication of the difficulties a commander must have had in fulfilling the post's missions, but there were other indications as well.

In April 1867 the commander of the District of New Mexico issued orders to all the posts that due to the lack of men only the headquarters at Santa Fe could approve escort missions.[14] The problem continued for in March 1870, Lieutenant Julian R. Fitch, 15th Infantry, complained to Santa Fe: "Only 9 men for duty", and "had to send Wagonmaster Perkins and teamsters to Fort Union without military escort."[15]

The post commanders also complained frequently against splitting up their meager forces by the establishment of outposts or pickets that had been ordered by Santa Fe. After several ambushes in the Organ Mountains, the headquarters in Santa Fe finally directed Fort Selden to establish an outpost or picket at San Augustine Spring. The spring, also known as Shedd's Ranch, was a favorite stopping point for travelers and wagon trains, but it was also favorite ambush area for bandits and Apaches. The spring was located on the east side of the Organ Mountains about twenty miles east of Las Cruces on the road to Alamogordo and Fort Stanton. When Major William B. Lane, 3rd Cavalry, was ordered by Santa Fe to establish a picket at Shedd's Ranch he replied 19 April 1869:

> . . . I have established the picket at Shedd's ranch . . . but can do nothing about the repeated acts of carelessness or foolishness, or stupidity of a portion of the people. Mr. Thomas who was killed was traveling alone and on mule over what is considered the worst Indian country in this vicinity. . . . [16]

Lane was obviously upset not only about the loss of his available manpower to this duty, but also about the foolhardiness of the travelers. Fort Selden must have removed the outpost when Lane departed, and this resulted in an outcry from the local citizenry. Brevet Lieutenant Colonel Frank Stanwood, 3rd Cavalry, commanding the post in October 1869 wrote headquarters:

> Messrs Shedd and Blake want a picket [outpost] established at San Augustine Springs . . . regarded by all as most dangerous area in this section of New Mexico . . . a good idea, but we do not have the manpower.[17]

However, the district commander sided with Messrs. Shedd and Blake and the outpost was re-established despite Stanwood's manpower shortages.

The commanders and officers at Fort Selden sent many messages through the years concerning the problems of low strength, but none reflected the frustration or were so terse as the words of Major Lane, 3rd Cavalry, who sent this response to a critical message from Santa Fe about the lack of training on 30 March 1869, "impossible to get over half of camp for the purpose of drill . . . they are gone on extra duty, daily duty, wood detail and guard mount." Lieutenant Oscar Elting, 3rd Cavalry, later in 1869 echoed these frustrations. "Troop K has only 13 privates present for duty . . . I cannot comply with directions [for escort duty received 4 October 1869 from Headquarters, District of New Mexico]. I do not have the men."[18] These messages reflect the frustrations of commanders trying to get a job done when they just did not have the resources.

The census of 1870 provides a snapshot of the makeup of the units at the post. There were 115 soldiers surveyed, which included three officers and 112 enlisted men. The post contingent at that time was two cavalry troops, G and I of the 8th Cavalry. There were no black troopers at Fort Selden during the census taking. A little over fifty per cent of the enlisted men were foreigners, who named Ireland, Switzerland, England, Prussia, Baden, Wurtzburg, Hannau, Hesse, Saxony, Canada, France, Bavaria, Poland, and Bosnia as their birthplaces. Ireland was the most frequently mentioned. The soldiers listing the United States as a birthplace were primarily from the Northeast and Midwest, though California, Missouri, Mississippi, and Kentucky were also represented.[19]

The quality of the troops at Fort Selden was undoubtedly similar to that of the rest of the army. The post had its fair share of hard workers, tough non-commissioned officers, hard drinkers, thieves, foreigners, gamblers, deserters, and sadly enough murderers. The officers and non-commissioned officers at Fort Selden were extremely concerned with the problems of discipline, which resulted in a large number of company punishment and court-martials. Lieutenant Colonel Nelson H. Davis, the Inspector General of the Department of New Mexico, conducted an inspection of the new fort in October 1865 and was very critical of the state of discipline. The results of the inspection were cited in a letter from General Carleton to Captain James H. Whitlock.

> There is reported to be a lax and loose state of discipline at your post and a disregard for military duty. The men visit their concubines or courtesans to gamble and indulge in whiskey drinking at a collection of jacals just off the reservation. You and your officers must see to it.[20]

Carleton's "collection of jacals" was in reference to the new town of Leasburg that has been previously mentioned as a sore spot with the commanders of the fort.

The least breach of discipline would result in a quick and sometimes stiff punishment. The standard charge preferred against the soldiers was "an act prejudicial to good order and military discipline."[21] A breach of military discipline was primarily defined as the failure to obey a lawful order. For example, Private William Lawler, Troop K, 3rd Cavalry, refused to sew bags for the company's cook on Christmas Eve. He was charged with the failure to obey a lawful order, fined ten dollars, confined at hard labor for one month, and made to carry a twenty-five pound log for four hours a day during his confinement.[22] Private George Jackson, Company K, 38th Infantry, refused to go on work detail claiming that he was sick. Sick or not, he too, was charged with "failure to obey," and was court-martialed. He was found guilty, fined twenty-five dollars, and given a written reprimand. Major Lane, the post commander, reviewed this court-martial record and wrote to the members of the court, ". . . this was an inadequate sentence. The prisoner was guilty of a positive disobedience of an order."[23]

Some of the charges of breaches of discipline made rather humorous reading, but obviously not to the soldier at the time. One soldier was fined and confined at hard labor for drinking out of a corporal's cup. Another soldier received the same sentence for throwing a piece of bread in the mess hall, possibly expressing his opinion of the food.[24] In both of these cases the post commander showed lenience and overrode the board's findings. And on October 10, 1868, the Post's records show that a private was fined and given ten days at hard labor for stealing a dress hat and giving away the feather trimming. The records do not disclose to whom he gave the feathers, but a major suspect might have been a girl in Leasburg. In some cases the charges seemed quite petty. Private Victor Hawkins, Troop K, 3rd Cavalry, who had asked for a second ration of bread, was found, ". . . guilty of conduct prejudicial to good order and confined at hard labor for 10 days."[25]

Desertion and absenteeism were rampant at Fort Selden and must have driven commanders crazy with the already existing problem of low strength. Privates, corporals, sergeants (both black and white), and officers were charged with deserting or leaving their posts without permission.[26] Court-martials for absenteeism occurred at an amazing rate. Fort Selden in the year 1868 held a post or garrison level court-martial every month with seven or eight soldiers being charged with absence without leave (AWOL). Considering the fact that those units only had 40 to 50 men assigned meant that approximately 20 per cent of the command was being court-martialed every month in1868.

Usually the absence was from taps to reveille, and ninety per cent of the absences were visits to the saloons, gambling places, and girls of Leasburg. The other absences occurred when soldiers left their duty stations for the local gold fields of Piños Altos and Kingston. The court generally gave the maximum sentence of forfeiture of pay for one month, confinement at hard labor for one month, and in the case of non-commissioned officers, reduction to the ranks.

Private John Williams, Company K, 38th Infantry, left his hospital room, where he was confined for an illness, and walked to his wife's quarters. She was one of the company's laundresses living in quarters at the north end of the hospital. Williams was found guilty of AWOL and was fined one month's pay.[27] Williams might have been checking up on his wife because three weeks earlier on 6 May 1869, First Sergeant

Joseph C. Rutherford was found drunk on duty at William's quarters. For this Rutherford was fined nineteen dollars and reduced to the rank of private, but Major Lane remitted the reduction.

The more serious charges of desertion with the intent to remain away from the place of duty were handled by special and general court-martials. The problem at Fort Selden was serious. Again, low pay, boredom, and the nearness of the goldfields at Piños Altos and Kingston seemed to be the primary reasons of departure. The closeness of an international boundary also caused problems for the command when soldiers crossed and took up residence in Mexico.[28] In August 1871 the Fort Selden commander sent a total of twelve messages to Headquarters, Fort Marcy, and nine had to do with deserters or their punishment which shows the amount of time that commanders had to spend on this problem.

Not only did men desert, but they also took with them their horses, saddles, weapons, and other military gear. One soldier deserted with a wagon and six-mule team. Lieutenant Davis, 9 September 1877, reported that Private Alexander Russell, 15th Infantry, left Fort Selden on 16 July with a six mule team loaded with medical supplies en route to Fort Stanton. Davis asked the post commander, ". . . rumor has it Russell deserted with team, Is it true?"[29] Another private from Company B, 1st New Mexico Infantry, not only took the mule team, weapon, and wagon, but also his family.[30] Some of the soldiers were quite resourceful in their methods of escape. One group floated and rowed down the Rio Grande toward El Paso. They did well until a snag overturned the boat about ten miles downstream. One man drowned, and the others surrendered to the Doña Ana County sheriff.[31] Another group of soldiers took their horses and equipment pretending to be in search of deserters. Major David R. Clendenin, 8th Cavalry, was most upset because they had convinced the quartermaster clerk to provide them with official forage orders.[32] These orders allowed them to obtain hay and oats for their horses at government expense while deserting.

Civilian employees also deserted. Henry Fields, a blacksmith with Troop A, 8th Cavalry, left the post with an army rifle, horse, and cartridge belt. He later turned himself in at Las Cruces.[33]

The desertion problem was so serious that the fort commanders actually offered bounties of thirty dollars or more for the return of the escapees. Major Lane paid Sergeant Michael Monahans, Troop F, 3d Cavalry, thirty dollars for apprehending Private Monroe Reynolds of the same unit.[34] Mr. Shedd, rancher at San Augustine Springs, on 15 June 1875, was asked for a receipt so that he could receive the reward for capturing a deserter from Troop F, 8th Cavalry. A message to the chief of police of El Paso in 1884 stated, "An Irish born private has deserted the post and is a cooper by trade. Thirty dollars paid on his return." Also in May 1885 the post commander was offering thirty dollars each for the arrest and return of two deserters in the Albuquerque area.[35] Even Captain MacArthur, 13th Infantry, was plagued with desertion, but he pursued deserters so relentlessly that he had the lowest desertion rate in the command.[36]

Murder by soldiers and of soldiers at Fort Selden and in the surrounding communities was an altogether too common occurrence. In January 1866 General Carleton ordered Privates Adam Maize and John Gregory, Troop K, 3rd Cavalry, transferred to civilian authorities to stand trial for murder. On 2 March 1866 the Santa Fe *New Mexican* reported that at a "fandango" in Leasburg two troopers from the 3rd Cavalry got into a fight, and one was stabbed to death. The same newspaper has a story on 3 November 1866 about two lieutenants who were involved in a gunfight. "Lieutenants Warner and Hazelhurst killed each other in a gunfight in the post commander's quarters." A fellow officer, Lieutenant J.H. Storey, who witnessed and participated in the aftermath of the incident, reported the event in more detail in a letter to his fiancée:

> ...A horrible accident occurred at the post yesterday, which resulted in the death of two of our officers. You will remember I mentioned in a previous letter that while crossing the plains I messed [ate] with Mrs. Warner, wife of Lieut. Warner of my Company. Warner suspicioned [sic] for some time past that Lieut. Fred Hazelhurst of my regiment was too intimate with his wife.

Yesterday morning Johnny [Warner] called me into his room, locked the doors and handed me three letters addressed to his wife, written by Hazelhurst (professing his love for Julia)....He then went out to see the Colonel. About 12-1/2 o'clock I heard several pistol shots next door in the Colonel's quarters. As I was officer of the day I rushed out to ascertain the cause. Hazelhurst exclaimed "Oh my God, Storey, I am killed." So I went after Warner, just as I turned the corner of the building, I came across him. Poor fellow he was breathing his last—shot through the heart. Hazelhurst lived until five this morning. I remained with him all night poor fellow. The officers did not have much sympathy for him and thought he had but got his just desserts. I could not see the poor fellow die without a white face around him, so I remained with him to the last.[37]

The soldiers also killed civilians. On 18 September 1868 Leandro Bernardo, a teamster for the 15th Infantry, was found in the Rio Grande about a mile south of the fort. Two privates from Company A, 38th Infantry were arrested and charged with murder, their claim was that they had mistaken the unfortunate victim for an Indian raider.[38]

Murders continued to plague the commanders of Fort Selden even to its closing days. Private Samuel Carson, Company B, 10th Infantry, was murdered and his body thrown into the acequia (irrigation ditch) in Doña Ana in June 1888. The post surgeon reported that he was given, ". . . a Christian burial in the Post Cemetery."[39] The last reported murder occurred in 1890 only months before the post was closed. Lieutenant James E. Brett, 24th Infantry, the last commander of Fort Selden, reported, "Sergeant Scott killed Private John Hobson by striking him on the head with a club." The paymaster had just visited the post, and the men were gambling in the barracks. Sergeant Scott had won about eighty dollars of Hobson's money, and words were exchanged. According to Brett's report, "Scott struck him a cowardly and unjustifiable blow on the back of the head."[40]

One murder of a local that concerned Fort Selden's personnel was that of the Mescalero Apache Chief, Candetta, in late 1872.[41] He had been in La Mesilla testifying in the United States Circuit Court and had left for Mescalero Reservation. He and his interpreter Juan Coja were found in Canyon La Luz. Major Clendenin fearing the death of Candetta would lead to an outbreak of the Apaches went with thirty troopers to the site. He reported that there were, ". . . indications of a severe struggle . . .," and that Candetta had gone into the mountains. Nerves were rather jittery for some time over this murder for fear of Apache reprisals. The *Weekly New Mexican*, 10 December 1872, reported that the interpreter had stabbed Candetta and Candetta killed Coja before he died. That finding closed the case but it would be interesting to see how many people of the time actually believed it, especially those in Mescalero.

Accidents also seemed to claim a number of lives at the post. Captain Ellis reported the loss of the bugler of Company D, 13th Infantry. He had been accidentally shot by a private coming in from a hunting trip.

> . . . had gone out hunting using the company shotgun. Gun had been cleared but the private saw a hawk, reloaded his gun, then didn't clear it before entering the barracks. . . . He picked it up to clean it, and it discharged severing the musician's carotid artery. The musician was cleaning gear getting ready for retreat parade.[43]

In another incident the *New Mexican*, 5 June 1871, reported the death of Charles Hayes, Company C,[Troop C, 8th Cavalry] due to an accidental overdose of "nicotine or some stupefying drug."

Even with all the loss of man power due to murders, accidents, and desertions, drunkenness seemed to be the biggest problem for the commanders at Fort Selden. It was not only a problem in itself, but it created other bad situations such as the drunk soldier or officer missing the departure of his troop or company, fighting in the barracks and other places, insolence to non-commissioned officers and officers, and inability to perform duty.

First Sergeant John W. Williams, Company K, 38th Infantry,

previously mentioned as charged with AWOL from the hospital, was so drunk that he could not conduct reveille and was reduced from first sergeant to the rank of private.[44] Another sergeant was reduced in rank for stopping for a drink in Dona Ana, while coming in from patrol. He claimed that he was looking for his gun that had fallen from his holster. The board found him guilty of deserting his column.[45] Private Henry Duvall, Troop K, 3rd Cavalry, failed to report for a patrol. After being found drunk behind the bake house, he was court-martialed and found "guilty of actions prejudicial to good order."[46] Private John Mitchell, 3rd Cavalry, was accused of drunkenness and striking the servant of the post commander. His comment to the court-martial board, "the man's nose commenced to bleed, what caused it I don't know," must have irritated the court. He was fined a month's pay, confined at hard labor for one month, and ordered to carry a twenty-pound log from reveille to retreat for thirty days.[47]

Captain Joseph G. Tilford, 3rd Cavalry, writing to headquarters in March 1868 on his problems with Leasburg and drunken soldiers noted that:

> Private Johnson acted in such a mutinous manner I punished him on the spot. . . . old sinner Hackney [Judge A. H. Hackney of Las Cruces, partner of Adolphe Lea] poisoned first their stomachs with bad whiskey then their minds with still worse advice.[48]

Tilford did not indicate what punishment he had imposed so spuriously, but the incident indicates the frustration commanders experienced with having soldiers drunk on duty and having the saloons of Leasburg on the post's reservation. Another example of rapid punishment occurred in 1876. Lieutenant Casper A. Conrad, 15th Infantry, reported that his dispatch rider arrived, "so drunk he could barely stand up and had lost the dispatch, saddle, blanket, and arms. Confined at once."[49]

Enlisted men were not the only offenders with alcohol. General Carleton wrote to Captain Whitlock in April 1865 about one of Whitlock's subordinates, "Lieutenant John Oliphant is too intemperate to be a good officer . . ." In another instance, the post commander on 22 October 1875 was forced to confine one of his lieutenants to house arrest for missing duty, being drunk and disorderly, and trying to leave Fort Selden. In 1885 Captain MacArthur, 13th Infantry, reported that one of his officers was subject to, "exceedingly paroxysms of intoxification and was utterly worthless."[50] That kind of comment on his efficiency report would insure that he did not get promoted.

To combat the loss of manpower due to drinking, in 1871 Lieutenant Colonel Thomas C. Devin, 8th Cavalry, and his officers formed a temperance lodge to slow the drunkenness at the fort. The Las Cruces *Borderer* reported that the lodge had increased from twenty members to forty-three by March, and that it was designed "to keep them out of trouble on payday."[51]

Historian William Leckie reported that Buffalo Soldiers had a lower court-martials rate for drunkenness and desertion than did comparable white cavalry units across the army.[52] This statement did not seem to hold true for the black soldiers at Fort Selden. A review of the Fort Selden court-martial records for 1867 to 1873 showed that the rates were similar for both black and white soldiers. Both groups were caught going to Leasburg in approximately equal numbers, and both groups received severe punishment for their transgressions.

Yet with all the desertion, drunkenness, and other problems facing the commanders and soldiers, the units at Fort Selden resolutely held to their duty. The misbehavior at Fort Selden was probably a reflection of the violent frontier society as a whole rather than the poor quality of manpower stationed at the post. The local press reported shootings, knifings, and drunkenness as daily occurrences in the local communities, so Fort Selden was not alone with these types of social problems.

The basic problem with research of events from the messages sent by commanders is that they generally reported only on those actions out of the ordinary. The fact that thirty privates did their duty in an honorable and brave manner on a particular day would not be reported, while the one or two who got in trouble would be.

One soldier's name that did appear in the messages which

provides an indication of the fortitude and sense of duty that most of the men must have had was that of Bugler Jacob Bath. Bath, a fifty-seven year-old private in Company B, 13th Infantry, had served in the regiment his entire career and was on his fourth enlistment. He began having problems with his teeth in 1882 that prevented him from blowing the bugle. He went to a dentist in Santa Fe at his own expense, but the false teeth provided were worthless for his primary duty of musician. Captain Gustavus M. Bascom, 13th Infantry, pleaded with his Headquarters: ". . . cannot something be done for this loyal, faithful old soldier."[53] Apparently not, for the post was reportedly reduced to sounding its bugle calls with a cook's triangle. In April 1883, a new musician was recruited, and on 8 May 1883, Jacob Bath received an honorable discharge for his long service with the 13th Infantry. This was not a particularly happy ending for Jacob Bath, but the vignette provides good insight into the dedication of troops that served at Fort Selden, the majority of whom quietly served honorably and faithfully.

As for the non-commissioned officers, Don Ricky stated, "If a single word were chosen to describe the non-commissioned officer of the Indian wars army, that word would have to be tough."[54] Sergeant T. V. Gibson, 13th Infantry, recognized his own toughness on his return from duty at Fort Selden in 1883:

> When our company came into Wingate from 4 years in the field along the border of New Mexico and Arizona. . . . The boys at Fort Wingate sure gave us a big blow out and the band met us on the mountain . . . we sure were a hard looking bunch when we arrived from old Fort Selden on the Rio Grande in New Mexico."[55]

### Sanitation

The post surgeon or his representative, the hospital steward, and the Inspector General, saw to the post's sanitation and health, which was ultimately the responsibility of the commander, by their monthly and annual inspections. They inspected the barracks, kitchens, sinks (latrines), laundry, and even the corrals, and reported to the post commander and the higher headquarters the status of the areas. The reports were not always glowing.

The odor in the new barracks must have been rather strong for the Inspector General in his report in 1865 stated, "bedding needs to be aired at least three times a week and the barracks washed."[56] Again in 1875 the post surgeon commented, ". . . blankets and bedding must be aired once a week"[57] The odor must have persisted for he complained in a subsequent report, "Men only bathe once a week in the river. Recommend large bathtubs be procured one for each company, and the men instructed to attend to personal cleanliness."[58] There was no evidence that the commanders or quartermaster ever ordered bathtubs, but a bathhouse was built in 1885 over the hot springs about a mile northwest of the post.

Other areas of the post received their fair share of derogatory comments. The guard house was inspected in May 1875, ". . . cells need disinfectant and deodorizing." Another report was on the laundry, the laundresses must have been tossing their wastewater out the front door onto the parade field. The commander issued an order, "The Officer of the Day should check the laundresses once a week to insure wash water is thrown away from the door."[59] The latrines though, received the most comments. "Sinks seats and floors need to be swept daily and washed once a week" was a common report, and there were also lectures to the commander and first sergeants about the use of lime and how often it should be used for proper sanitation.[60]

The surgeon was very upset after inspecting the corrals. He reported to the commander, there is, "evidence that the men are using the corrals as privies."[61] He also found this in the barracks, "Some filthy creatures have been urinating in the room containing the company's water barrels."[62] One would like to think that these last two comments were brought about by excessive alcohol consumption and not customary acts. Most of the monthly reports from the doctor and his representative about the overall condition of the fort ended upbeat and complimentary, but there were many negative reports on the water used by the post. The problems with the water sanitation are discussed in Chapter 4.

## Black and White Relations

Another problem that arose on Fort Selden was racial bias. Black troops such as the 125th Infantry, 38th Infantry, 24th Infantry, and the 9th Cavalry were stationed at Fort Selden for approximately one-third of the post's life. The infantry, because of its lack of mobility in what has been described as a mobile war, was used in a support role. The infantryman rarely went on patrols; he guarded the herds and corrals, provided escort to the mail when transportation was available, and generally was used on post details. The cavalry was used as a mobile strike force and did most of the actual fighting. In the early days of the post the black infantry supported white cavalry, but with the arrival of the 9th Cavalry in the late 1870s the roles reversed. The Buffalo Soldiers were now defending Hispanic and Anglo settlers from the marauding Apaches, while being supported by the white infantrymen. This created an interesting situation considering the prejudices of the times.

The Las Cruces *Thirty-Four* was extremely vocal against the black soldier. Articles contained statements such as, "A thousand white soldiers and General MacKenzie is what we need . . . The climate seems to be getting too hot for the 9th . . . hope the 9th will be sent to Dakota to cool off."[63] Another article in February 1880 lamented that Major Albert P. Morrow, 9th Cavalry, conducting operations against Victorio, had only 300 white soldiers, while the rest were black. The article went on to say, "If Morrow had the same quality of troops as General Crook our Indian problems would be over."[64]

There were some unfortunate incidents between black and white individuals on the post, but not to the extent that it created major problems, such as the mutiny at Fort Cummings or the dancehall murders at Fort Bayard. Compared to these incidents Fort Selden was rather quiet. One of the incidents was an argument that occurred in May 1867 during a detail that contained both black and white soldiers. Private Henry Clark, Troop K, 3rd Cavalry, and Private Wilson Owen, Company I,

125th Infantry, got into a fracas that resulted in a court-martial for Clark. Clark believed that he had been insulted by the black soldier. He stated, "You black son of a bitch I will split your brains out," and hit him with a shovel.[65] Clark was found guilty of assault and punished. On 2 July 1869 musician Lawrence Mason, Company K, 38th Infantry, was charged with AWOL. He had been on duty as the Adjutant's runner and had asked the clerk for and received permission to be gone for 10 minutes, but left for the day. The clerk called him a "goddamned black sow"[66] Mason was found guilty and had to forfeit one month's pay. There is no evidence of punishment for the clerk for his language. Mason had a hard time staying out of trouble in Leasburg, because at another court-martial, 15 September 1868, he was accused and found guilty of being in Leasburg without permission and was fined and forced to carry a log for fifteen days. Another racial incident occurred in 1876. The telegraph operator returning to Fort Selden in a drunken condition refused to respond to the black soldier on guard. The officer in charge arrested the operator because, "He called the guard a nigger and asserted his superiority as a white man."[67]

Don Ricky noted that "even at small garrisons, composed of one company of infantry and one of cavalry, the tendency was for the men of one unit to have little contact with those of the other."[68] This was the case at Fort Selden. Though there were some incidents of racial problems, generally the units at Fort Selden had very little contact with each other, whether by plan or accident. The units had separate mess halls, separate barracks, the cavalry was away from the post on patrol a good deal of the time, and usually, the post work details were segregated by unit. The racial problems habitually occurred in Leasburg, Las Cruces, or La Mesilla during off duty time.

**Civilian Staffing and the Distaff**

In addition to the military staffing of Fort Selden civilians provided many necessary services to the post. Throughout the twenty-six year history of the post civilians provided continuity as clerks, guides, and members of the quartermaster's office. This staff did not change when the units rotated to another post.

The number of civilians hired at Fort Selden varied from year-to-year because hiring depended upon the availability of federal funds. In 1867 the quartermaster at Fort Selden was authorized to hire a clerk, forage master, wheelwright, carpenter, two saddlers or packers, blacksmith, and a wagon master.[69] In addition to these, the hospital hired a matron, and each of the companies hired company laundresses. Typically these ladies were wives of soldiers assigned to the unit, but local girls were also hired. The census of 1870 showed that of the three laundresses employed at the post, two were soldier's wives.

Other local civilians were hired for specific tasks, such as repairing the mud ovens, guiding the patrols, plastering the ever-eroding walls, and repairing the leaky roofs. Brevet Lieutenant Colonel Frank Stanwood, 3rd Cavalry, requested permission to hire a guide, Juan Arroyez, to operate a scout from the post in November 1869. In 1884 Captain MacArthur, 13th Infantry, pleaded with district headquarters for funds to hire a mason: ". . . even the smallest sum will help the barracks . . . only $40 on hand."[70]

Sometimes there was a shortage of civilian personnel in addition to the perennial shortage of soldiers. Lieutenant Colonel Devin, 8th Cavalry, asking for more funds for the post in 1871, reported that he, "Still need a mason to repair damages. . . . Down to two civilian employees, the quartermaster clerk, and the blacksmith."[71] More funding must have been made available because the post returns in 1886 showed as civilian employees two teamsters, two plasterers, two laborers, and a clerk.

The wives of officers and enlisted men also provided necessary staffing to the post. With the arrival of the regulars after the Civil War, women also came to Fort Selden. They tended the sick, educated the children, raised vegetables and other foods, and provided relief from the dull routine of military duties. The ladies hosted picnics, outings, and dances, which tended to enliven post life somewhat.[72] The Fort Selden wives also, had teas and "socials" which included the officers of the post. Mrs. Tilford invited the officers and wives of the command to a tea in October 1867. "Mrs. Tilford requests the pleasure of your company to social tea this evening."[73] Several messages also referred to band concerts and singing in the evening.

Lydia Spencer Lane reported only four other women at the post in 1869, but according to her, they were not too friendly. Still she did pat herself on the back for her butter and egg production.

> My churn was primitive . . . a large stone jar that held three gallons. A soldier carpenter made the top and the dasher from rough pine . . . with no ice or cold spring water to chill the butter was like oil when freshly churned, but I was able to churn 150 pounds.[74]

She added that even though she had problems with coyotes, her chickens prospered. "Our table was well supplied with eggs and chicken."[75]

Other women taught school or provided other types of volunteer social work. The saddler's wife was hired in 1884 to teach the first school formally organized at Fort Selden. She taught the post's thirteen children in the day and illiterate soldiers in the evening.[76]

The wives and women of the post were also willing performers during emergencies. When a dreadful diphtheria epidemic swept the fort in 1886 Lieutenant and Mrs. William N. Hughes, 13th Infantry, lost two of their children, Linda Belle, four years of age, and Sara, four months old. The women pitched in and did most of the consoling and cleaning. Captain MacArthur and his son Douglas were also extremely sick.[77] The post surgeon with the post's women's help fumigated the rooms, burned articles of clothing, and washed their living areas with white lime. They also took over the responsibility of cooking and caring for the sick for the rest of those affected.

## Diversions

Fort Selden did not offer much in off-duty entertainment. Mrs. Lane offered this observation, ". . . . it was indeed, a dull little place for entertainment. We rode a great deal, but Indian scares kept us within a mile or so of camp."[78] A Fort Union soldier also commented on the boredom, "How intolerably dull and monotonous it is to be penned up in a Frontier Military Post on a Sunday . . . not even a Sabbath School or anything else to engage or divert the mind."[79] Fort Selden's soldiers faced long rides to make it to church in Doña Ana, Las Cruces or La Mesilla.

They did ride, hunt, and fish, but the primary diversion then was a trip to Leasburg's grog shops for drinking, dancing, and gambling. Gambling in the barracks, if caught, meant swift punishment, but soldiers were persistent in their gambling habits. Sergeant Oliver Cook was caught playing cards in the barracks by the officer-of-the-day and placed in barracks arrest, but he broke arrest and was found later in the water closet engaged in another game of cards.[80] Another group was caught playing cards in the post bake house.[81] A fandango in Leasburg ended in tragedy in 1866, "On the night 17 February at a Fandango in this place [Leasburg] Dick Reynolds stabbed and killed a man by the name of Hendricks, both soldiers belonging to M Company[troop] of the Cavalry [New Mexico Volunteers]."[82]

For the literate, reading must have been one of the major forms of recreation because the list of periodicals was quite impressive. The adjutant in 1869 reported that the post had received packages of periodicals to be distributed to the troops through the Service Library Association.[83] Captain MacArthur, 13th Infantry, reported that among others the post currently received, "*The Army and Navy Register, Harpers Weekly*, and *Puck*."[84] The saddler's wife had 20 or so illiterate soldiers in evening school, but MacArthur wanted a soldier for that duty. He requested a "Selected man be assigned to Company K as a teacher . . . as extra duty. . . . Wages to be 35 cents a day paid by the parents."[85] He did not receive the requested enlisted man though because in September he reminded Washington of his previous message.[86]

The soldiers did enjoy music and games. Mrs. Lane informs us that the post had a melodean, ". . . that created mournful, grunty, wheezy music."[87] One commander seemed to resent the singing and dancing of his officers, ". . . during my absence a number of people gathered on your porch singing and dancing until very late at night."[88] The soldiers' games seemed hampered by the same weather that affected their patrols. The traditional Fourth of July ballgame in 1883 between the 13th Infantry and 4th Cavalry was called after 3 innings, "it was too hot to run."[89]

The soldiers might have enjoyed relaxation by soaking in a hot mineral bath as one commander reported, "Private John McGrath has constructed a bathhouse at a mineral springs on the Post."[90] Diversions though on the whole seemed few and far between. One diversion by the soldiers was reported by the *Rio Grande Republican* on page 2, 7 July 1883, "Several large tarantulas were caught this evening and deposited upside down on ant beds . . . takes generally 10 to 15 minutes for ants to get rid of the legs." Questions arise, was this a scientific experiment or wagering event, or just sheer boredom?

Even with all its personnel shortages, drunkenness, and misbehavior, Fort Selden was probably no worse off than any other small frontier post in the southwest. Though inadequately staffed most of the time they still seemed to get their duties accomplished. The soldiers of Fort Selden both black and white, the women, and civilians of Fort Selden working together through the heat, dust, and immensity of the southwestern desert accomplished the military mission of protecting the region, and at the same time contributed to the growth and prosperity of the surrounding communities.

*Soldiers at Fort Selden, 1885, courtesy*
*Palace of the Governors Photo Archives (NMHM/DCA), 014523*

*Field gun at Fort Selden*

# 3

# The Conduct of Military Operations

The military field operations performed by the soldiers at Fort Selden probably had the most direct effect on the settlement and pacification of the area. These field operations, directed for the most part against the Apaches, included routine scouts (patrols), picket (outpost) duty, escort missions, and reactive combat operations. Other military operations, such as the establishment of communications systems and the daily fatigue details of the fort, though important were more indirect with their effects on the local communities. The Fort Selden logistical operations, which also impacted heavily on the local communities' economic growth, will be discussed in Chapter 4.

The soldiers at Fort Selden looked forward to getting away from the post and breaking the monotony of post details, though many of their missions were not all that exciting. Routinely, they left the post to escort individuals, freight wagons, cattle herds, and stagecoaches along the trails and roads in their area of responsibility, to conduct routine patrols, and to serve as members of an outpost. Yet, even on patrol a soldier's life was not easy, nor totally free from boredom. The immense distances of the southwestern landscape and the guerrilla form of warfare, raids and ambushes employed by the Apache warriors, created severe problems for soldiers. They also had to contend with bad rations, the difficult terrain, the lack of water, and at times; extreme heat, cold, dust, and bad weather. But all of these hardships were forgotten or ignored in the several minutes of adrenaline packed excitement of the short-lived firefights.

## Patrol and Scout Operations

The patrol was the tactic most frequently used by the army to keep hostile Native Americans on reservations or to chase them back onto the reservation. Lieutenants or non-commissioned officers usually led Fort Selden's patrols, but in some instances the company commander or even the regimental commander took the field. A non-commissioned officer assisted the patrol leader and the patrol would be comprised from as many men as the command could muster. The post commander planned the patrol route in advance and usually provided a civilian guide in those cases where the route was not familiar to the men. Captain Henry Carroll, 9th Cavalry, went so far as to tell headquarters that patrols were worthless without guides. Carroll said in a message in July 1876 that "without a guide a patrol is of little consequence . . . those nine or ten troops might as well remain on post."[1] So, he hired local Pueblo Indians on several missions as guides.[2] Captain Edmund Fechet, Troop C, 8th Cavalry, had a different opinion of guides according to the local newspaper. "Fechet out on a scout toward the Florita [Florida] Mountains failed to find Indians . . . deceived by his guide"[3]

The army units had a standing operating procedure (SOP) outlining how the unit would conduct field operations, and what equipment a man would carry on patrol in addition to his weapon and ammunition. Each unit that came into Fort Selden had a slightly different SOP but generally each required a soldier to have a minimum of two canteens, a blanket, and a skillet in addition to his rations on a patrol. The instructions, given to the men prior to departure of the patrol, were similar to current doctrine on briefing and debriefing patrol leaders. General Carleton gave these instructions to a patrol going out against the Mimbres Apache:

Proceed with great caution without noise of trumpet or drums or loud talking, or firing of guns except in battle . . . to march silently, mostly by night, to build fires of dry twigs so that no smoke may rise from them . . . to have no fires by night. . . . Kill every Indian man you can find. [You must] use pack mules where wagons cannot go.[4]

Captain Carroll, 9th Cavalry, also provided us with an excellent snapshot of the instructions routinely given to the patrol leaders and in this case, he directed both the speed of the patrol and the distance to cover:

Your scouting ordinary march should not exceed twenty miles a day but on trails there should be no limit except the endurance of your animals.

PS. If the Indian Agent at Ojo Caliente calls for assistance you will use all force at your command.[5]

Fort Selden's commanders used the patrol both as a reconnaissance operation to gain intelligence on hostile bands and the land, or as a deterrent, a show of force with the objective of keeping or putting the renegades back on the reservation. Some patrols were as boring as the routine camp life, especially if the enemy was not encountered. On 5 April 1866 Captain (Brevet Major) William Brady, 1st New Mexico Cavalry, filed this report of a routine patrol to Fort Bliss:

1st day: left this post with Lieutenant M. Carrigan and 25 enlisted men of Companies A and H, 1st NM Cavalry . . . scouted east to San Augustine Springs. No sign of Indian.

2d day: moved north to San Nicholas Springs [in the San Andres Mountains], high winds, no sign of Indians.

3d day: Rejoined Lt Carrigan at San Augustine Springs. no Indians.

4th day: Followed the old wagon road to rocky springs.

5th-7th Day: moved south down the east slope, scouting toward

Fort Bliss, very hot.

8th day: arrived at Fort Bliss.

9th day rested horses and mules.

10th day: marched at 6 AM. . . arrived cottonwood springs [Near present site of Anthony, NM on the Rio Grande] at 3, covered 25 miles.

11th day: weather cold with rain and hail departed 6 AM arrived Las Cruces 10 PM.

12th day: Departed Las Cruces 8 AM. Arrived Fort Selden 2 PM. No sign of Indians total distance covered 183 miles.[6]

It seems that the weather, with high winds, sand, hot and cold temperatures, rain, and hail, was the most challenging part of this patrol.

Other patrol reports were not quite so dull, yet were still terse. The brevity of such reports leaves it to the reader's imagination to fill in the powder smells, the battle cries of the combatants, the dust, and the unmistakable sound of bullet striking flesh followed by the moans of the wounded or the absolute silence of the dead. Lieutenant Storey made this report to Major C. H. DeForrest, headquarters, District of New Mexico in September 1866:

I have the honor to submit the following report; in accordance with S.O. [Special Orders] 94 dated HQ, Fort Selden Sept 8th 1866. I left this post with twelve men Co I, 125th U.S.C.I.[Unites States Colored Infantry] mounted on mules with ten days rations on a scout against a party of Indians supposed to be in the vicinity of the San Andreas [sic] Mountains, Organ Range. Sep 8th, 1st day. Left the post at 5 o'clock P.M. traveled 25 miles East, made a dry camp on the prairie at 12 o'clock midnight. Good Grass, no wood or water. Distance traveled 25 miles.

Sept 9th-Broke camp at Daybreak. Travelled 20 miles. Camped at a spring known as the Caresa in the foothills of the San Andreas, where I met a party of eight citizens, 3 Americans and 5 Mexicans, to cooperate with me. . . . scouted the San Augustine area from the San Andreas canyon to San Augustine Springs, found no fresh signs or tracks. Distance traveled 25 miles. Sept 10th Broke camp at 6 o'clock A.M. traveled NNE to Jones Lead in San Andreas canyon, where I left a sufficient guard for my animals and with ten men ascended Padre Peak and passed over to the east side of the mountains. On a ledge about 1,000 feet below the peak, I discovered a vein of argentiferous galena with good indications of silver.[7]

Storey proceeded to spend the next two days mining and assaying the ore. He was finally forced to quit when they broke the only rock drill they had with them. He then continued on his scout to the northeast stopping when he ran into a party of thirty-five Apaches. According to his after action report he could not get the citizens to assist him in going up against the "Rancheria" so he and his party returned to Fort Selden. He left the citizens at the entrance to the canyon, ". . . where they were to commence operations on the San Andreas [San Andres] silver mine".[8] On the evidence, it would seem that the target of this scout was silver, not Apaches.

Captain George W. Chilson of Troop C, 8th Cavalry, submitted a more aggressive patrol report on 17 July 1873:

Left post with ten mounted men on 9 Jul ultimo chasing Indians who had stolen horses from Shedd's ranch. . . .After following them for 4 1/2 days . . . caught them west of Cañada Alamosa. I report the loss of Corporal Frank Brauting [Battling]. Three Indians killed. The stock recovered. Distance covered 350 miles.[9]

If he submitted his report on the day after he arrived back at Fort Selden, Chilson covered the 350 miles in eight days. He and his patrol must have been tired for they averaged over forty miles a day. Historian Dan Thrapp reported that in this Cañada Alamosa battle, Corporal Frank Battling was killed, and "three troopers, First Sergeant James L. Morris, Sergeant Leonidas Lytle, and Private Henry Mills", were awarded the Congressional Medal of Honor.

One routine patrol ended in a mystery. Captain Gerald Russell, 3rd Cavalry, left Fort Selden on 11 August 1868, with forty men, twenty from Company K, 38th Infantry, and twenty from Troop K, 3rd Cavalry. This is one of those rare instances that combined black and white troops on the same patrol. The patrol rode north toward Palomas Creek, which flows east out of the Black Range about sixty miles north of Fort Selden. They planned to cross the Black Range and scout the Mimbres Valley. On 14 August in the Palomas Creek bed they encountered a twenty-man wood gathering patrol from Fort McRae (a sister fort now covered by the waters of Elephant Butte Reservoir) that reportedly had been attacked by 100 Apaches. This report is suspect because the Apache never had war parties that large. The leader of the McRae patrol was a civilian named Ellis, the post quartermaster clerk. Ellis had been badly wounded, so his patrol returned to McRae. The Fort Selden patrol continued west into the Black Range following the trail of the hostiles. Darkness followed by a terrible downpour of rain and hail obscured the trail, but the patrol continued toward the Mimbres Valley through Emory Pass. As was the custom during rest stops or night halts, pickets or guards were positioned away from the main body to provide security and early warning for the patrol. Private Richard B. Baker, Troop K, 3rd Cavalry, was one such guard. On his return to the main body he discovered that he had left his pistols back at his security position. When he went to retrieve the pistols, he disappeared. A search of the area produced no clues, and Baker was reported as a combat loss.[11] Questions immediately arise as to why a quartermaster clerk was commanding a patrol, why Baker was allowed to go by himself to retrieve his pistols, and what happened to him? The patrol report remains mute on all three questions.

Not all patrols were successful, nor did cooperation between forts always occur when it was needed. A major expedition of over 200 men against Apaches in southeastern New Mexico and west Texas led by Major Alexander Moore, 38th Infantry, in April and May 1869 had stripped Fort Selden of all but a few soldiers. Major William B. Lane, then commanding Fort Selden, asked Fort Bliss to assist him with a scout into the Franklin and Organ Mountains. The Fort Bliss commander must have responded halfheartedly for Lane's subsequent message was rather acerbic.

> I am sorry that the 35th Infantry gave up. The idea that sending a force from another district might embarrass the district of New Mexico is ridiculous. We are all U.S. troops and the Indians are U.S. Indians and deserve all the thrashing the troops can give them.[12]

With respect to Major Lane, I hardly think that the Apaches considered themselves "U.S. Indians" at that time, but I can understand his frustration that a sister fort responded so feebly to his request for help with his operation.

Another interesting aspect of the post's field operations was the sharing of captured material as spoils among the members of the patrol. In 1876 Captain Carroll, 9th Cavalry, led a successful scout into the Florida Mountains of southwestern New Mexico chasing an unknown number of hostile Apaches. The patrol captured eleven ponies, killed one Apache, and wounded three others, with one cavalryman, Private Harrison Bland, wounded. The ponies were later sold for $100, and the money was split among the troops on the patrol.[13]

The patrol continued to be the primary combat operation until the closure of the fort. However, the most frantic of the Post's operations was the response to raids and ambushes.

**Responses to Raids and Ambushes**

The combat operations organized and dispatched as a reaction to hostile acts were more hectic than routine reconnaissance patrols. An example of a reaction operation was Fort Selden's first combat mission. An express rider from General Carleton arrived on 20 June 1865 from Fort Marcy with the following orders:

> A number of Navahos [Navajos] have broken out [from Bosque Redondo] . . . make all attempts to capture or destroy . . . send all

mounted men to Fort Craig at once. Take an abundant supply of ammunition. . . . Prevent their crossing of the Rio Grande.[14]

The twenty or so mounted troops from Fort Selden made a forced march toward Fort Craig some ninety miles to the north, but the Navajos returned to the reservation before the troops reached Fort Craig. This episode ended without conflict, but other incidents were not so peaceful.

Another example of a reactive mission demonstrated how cooperation between the forts was supposed to work. General Carleton ordered Captain Joseph G. Tilford and Troop K, 3rd Cavalry, to Dog Canyon in the Sacramento Mountains near Alamogordo to assist units from Fort Union who were chasing a small band of Mescalero Apaches.

> 20-40 Indians attacked Mora . . . send Company [troop] K with wagons, supplies, forage and subsistence to Dog Canyon and scout the country. Arrive 5 October to cooperate with soldiers of Fort Union to punish these Indians. Destroy all male adult Indians capable of bearing arms.[15]

The combined force chased the Apaches through the Sacramento Mountains and south into Texas where units coming north from Fort Davis, Texas joined the fray. The Santa Fe *New Mexican* labeled this patrol a "successful Indian fight" as it captured many horses, drove the Indians out of the territory, and had only two soldiers wounded.[16] Carleton's message also highlighted his standard order to his subordinates of "no quarter" to the Native Americans who had left the reservation. It is to the credit of the officers and men of Fort Selden that Carleton's order of "no quarter" was ignored.

Stolen horses and cattle were the cause of many reactive combat operations. District headquarters, in May 1866 ordered troops from Fort Selden to the San Andres to "cut" the trail of a party of Apaches that had stolen sixty-eight mules and horses from Jesus Baca.[17] In September 1866 a Native American raiding party killed the hay cutter and drove off the herd and work oxen belonging to Fort Selden. The Santa Fe *New*

*Mexican* reported that, "Lieutenant Billings gallantly made a charge with 6 or 7 troopers into the very midst of a large party of Indians, 60 or 70, recovering the stock."[18] The post herd seemed to be a favorite target because it was hit again in November 1867 when Apaches ran off with forty horses, but were surprised by the quick reaction of the Fort Selden cavalry and the herd was recovered.[19]

Shedd's ranch also seemed to be a favorite target. Captain Gerald Russell, 3rd Cavalry, left the post on 19 November 1868 with twenty five men from Troop K to recapture horses stolen from Shedd's Ranch. They followed the trail from the San Andres Mountains to the San Diego crossing of the Rio Grande about six miles north of the fort (also referred to as Tonuco Mountain) where twenty more troopers reinforced them. Russell then followed the trail to the Florida Mountains and to the Tres Hermanas Mountains northwest of present day Columbus, New Mexico, and only stopped when the trail led into Mexico. In January 1872 The *Borderer* reported, "two more horses stolen from Shedd's ranch. . . . [The fort's] scout followed them to a crossing near Chamberino . . . lost trail in the bottoms lands."[21] Major Clendenin, 8th Cavalry, reported in October 1876 that thirty animals belonging to a wagon train camped near Las Cruces were run off, he gave pursuit with thirty troopers. Some of the stock was recovered but he felt that it was probably "Mexican" horse thieves because they kept to the main post road after crossing the Organ Mountains.[22]

Apache raids on the communities caused the most virulent responses of the local newspapers to the seeming inability of the forces at Fort Selden to protect them. Even with their most diligent efforts the soldiers often seemed to be in the wrong place, and Apache raids continued to plague the Mesilla Valley until the early 1880s. Several raids hit close to home. In September 1865 they were in the right place when a cattle herd corralled about seven miles south of Las Cruces was stampeded, but thanks to the rapid response of Lieutenant Colonel Charles T. Jennings, Captain Whitlock, and Lieutenant Houston [1st New Mexico Volunteers] they were recovered the next morning.[23] A writer for the Santa Fe *New Mexican* in March 1869 seemed rather tired of the continuing raids on the post's stock when reporting yet another attack on the wood train by twenty-five Indians. "Only a miracle prevented total loss. . . . How a handful of naked, starving, savages should indefinitely beleaguer a military post so well appointed as Fort Selden is beyond our ken."[24] However, the papers also understood the importance of the fort. The *New Mexican* reported that a mule train had been attacked within the boundaries of the fort, "We can only imagine what depredations would occur if any of the forts be broken up."[25]

The frustration with the continuing attacks was directed not at the "valiant and brave soldiers," but at a government in Washington that refused to acknowledge the problem or to offer an acceptable solution.

> Within 7 days Apaches have captured 3 mails, taken stock, and killed two company drivers [Southern Overland Stage Company]. Why cannot the government do something? We cannot but look upon the parsimonious policy of the government in sending us a mere handful of troops as penny wise and pound foolish.[26]

Continuous patrolling throughout the region by Fort Selden's troops, led by Lieutenant Colonel Thomas C. Devin and Captain Edmund G. Fechet, both of the 8th Cavalry, during 1870–1872 paid dividends and slowed the Indian raids. The Santa Fe press reported in December 1871 that "Indian depredations are less frequent than formerly. . . . Our citizens in the southern portion of the territory enjoy almost complete immunity."[27] However, the peace was not to last.

In 1871 The Territorial Superintendent for Indian Affairs, Nathaniel Pope, and Colonel Gordon Granger, commander of the District of New Mexico after General Carleton's departure, began a policy of consolidation for the Mimbres and Southern Apache.[28] The first combined reservation was to be in the Tularosa Mountains (now part of the Gila National Forest and not to be confused with the town north of Alamogordo). It was located about eighty miles west of Ojo Caliente, the then homeland and reservation for the Mimbres Apaches (about three miles southeast of Dusty, N.M.) General Order Number 8, Headquarters,

Military Division of the Missouri, required that the soldiers gather and move all the associated Apaches to the new reservation in the Tularosa Valley.[29] The associated Apaches included the Mimbres, some Chiricahuas, Coyoteros, Gila, and Mogollon bands.[30]

The Tularosa effort lasted three years and was a dismal failure, so in 1874 a reservation was re-established at Ojo Caliente. The government policy of consolidation continued and in May 1876 the few Ojo Caliente Apaches who could be assembled were moved to the San Carlos reservation in Arizona. In September 1877 Victorio and his Mimbres Apaches left the San Carlos and returned to their homeland of the Black Range in southern New Mexico. They were soon causing havoc throughout the southwestern portion of New Mexico.[31] Units from Fort Selden and other posts chased the various leaders, Victorio, Loco, Pionsenay, Nana, and Chiva all over the southwestern desert. Pionsenay and the southern Apaches went to Mexico, while Victorio, Nana, and Loco ended up on the Mescalero reservation. Pope then decided to reopen the Ojo Caliente reservation and allow the Mimbres people to return to their homeland, but the decision was made too late to prevent the outbreak of Victorio's War.

Victorio, an Apache Chief, long feared in the Mesilla Valley, began his last desperate push to get the whites out of his area. The army had forced Victorio and about forty of his Ojo Caliente band onto the Mescalero Reservation in 1878, but incidents between the two tribes, plus a warrant for his arrest, sent him fleeing back toward the Black Range on 21 August 1879.[32] The commander of Fort Selden, Captain Henry Carroll, 9th Cavalry, was ordered with all available troopers to Ojo Caliente, where he joined the rest of the regiment under the command of Colonel Albert P. Morrow. With the troops in the field chasing Victorio for the next two years Fort Selden was temporarily abandoned and would not be reoccupied until 25 December 1880.[33] After Victorio's defeat in Mexico in 1880, small raids continued sporadically in the Mesilla Valley, but essentially the Apache threat was over. Geronimo's final outbreak from the San Carlos reservation in 1886 was to the west, and Fort Selden's troops were not involved except for the previously mentioned "be prepared to assist" message to Captain MacArthur.

A few reactive missions continued after the post was reopened in the 1880s. In August 1881 the commander at Fort Bayard requested that Fort Selden send every available man to Rincon "fully equipped and with 10 days rations" to assist Company J, 15th Infantry, chasing a band of Native Americans on the east side of the Black Range.[34] There were no follow up messages on this combined action, so it is not known if it was successful. Again, in April 1883 the district ordered a detachment of Troop B, 4th Cavalry, stationed at the outpost at Shedd's ranch, to "pick up the track" of Indians reported near the White Sands area, but the commander of the detachment was AWOL at the time, so it is not known if any attempt was made. The final mission of the post was sent in 1889. Lieutenant James Brett, 24th Infantry, sent a combat patrol into the San Andres Mountains against a small Apache band on 23 October 1889. The group was not located and this brought down the curtain on the combat operations against the Apaches from Fort Selden.

**Picket and Escort Duty**

Another type of mission was the outpost or picket. Fort Selden had two important outposts to protect travelers and to allow rapid reaction of troops within the most dangerous areas of the post's area of operations. By 1867 the post had established outposts at Aleman's station (also known as Martin's ranch, south of present day Engle) at the midpoint of the Jornada del Muerto, and at San Augustine Pass in the Organ Mountains. The latter outpost was actually located at Shedd's ranch on the east side of the mountains. The outpost strength was usually one non-commissioned officer with seven to ten privates. The outposts were mounted even when they were from an infantry unit, though on occasion commanders took away the men's horses to prevent them from deserting. The men at outposts were replaced every month to reduce the desertion rate, but the outposts always led the post in numbers of deserters probably due to boredom, the lack of supervision, and the availability of horses.[35]

The outposts received their share of raids and ambushes. Major Lane, 3rd Cavalry, had removed the picket from San Augustine Pass in early April 1869, due to a lack of troops. The result was an increased number of ambushes and deaths of citizens in the Organ Mountains. A previously mentioned ambush occurred during the night 17 April 1869 in San Augustine pass. Mr. Thomas was traveling alone through the pass with a herd of six horses when he was attacked. The next day Sergeant Adams, Troop K, 3rd Cavalry with twenty men found Thomas' body, stripped with an arrow in his neck.[36] On 2 May 1869 the remains of an Italian recluse were brought into La Mesilla. He had been killed in the Organ Mountains.[37]

Major Lane was then ordered by the district commander to reestablish the outpost. The newly established picket detail at Shedd's ranch was escorting Perfecto Armijo, a citizen of Las Cruces, westward through San Augustine Pass in May 1869 when they were ambushed. Corporal Charles Young was killed, Armijo and one other soldier wounded, but the party was able to return to Shedd's ranch.[38] An express rider, sent to carry the bad news to Fort Selden, rode through the pass a few hours later seeing no sign of hostiles. Captain Lawrence O'Connor, 3rd Cavalry, arrived the next morning with reinforcements from Fort Selden to look for Young's body and to hunt for the Indians. The body was recovered, but a scout of the area was unsuccessful.[39] Two more civilians were killed in San Augustine Pass in July 1869, but in this firefight the son held off the Apaches while his mother with a baby in her arms reached safety.[40] The pass continued to be very dangerous even after the post closure and responsibility for the area had passed to the county sheriff.

The picket at Aleman's Station continued until the arrival of the railroad in 1881. It was discontinued temporarily in September 1872 based on a complaint by Captain Fechet, 8th Cavalry. He wrote headquarters asking permission to remove the picket permanently because the fort had to pay to graze its horses on ranch land, and the nearness of Aleman's to Fort Selden made the picket unnecessary in his opinion.[41] But increased hostile activity in the area forced Colonel Granger, the District Commander, to reestablish the outpost in October 1872.[42]

The picket at Shedd's ranch continued until 1883. The last mission (previously mentioned) given to the outpost at Shedd's ranch was on 30 April 1883, "move north and strike the trail of Indians crossing the White Sands."[43] There is no evidence that this mission was ever executed because the commander of the outpost, the first sergeant of Troop B, 4th Cavalry, had left his post for El Paso. He was captured in El Paso and returned to duty on 23 July 1883.

The escort was the most enjoyable form of military operation for the soldiers of Fort Selden, especially if the assignment meant a trip to El Paso, Las Cruces, Albuquerque, or Santa Fe. The fort, even though short of men at times, provided escort to all forms of transportation and people moving through the area. In the Post Returns of 1866, some of the most common escort missions included escort for the freight wagons of Reynolds and Griggs of Las Cruces, the government paymaster, a government freight train to Fort Bliss, Isaac Jewitt and Robert Crandal's "small" train to Fort Cummings, and 800 head of cattle to Fort Bayard. One escort duty recorded by Lieutenant Storey in a letter to his fiancée did not sound too enjoyable.

> I arrived here [Fort Cummings] safely yesterday afternoon in the midst of a terrific thunderstorm. . . . I didn't enjoy it much. It is gloomy traveling in this country alone. . . . I traveled from Selden to Cummings with 5 wagons and 19 cattle. Made the trip 65 miles in 24 hours the last 40 miles without water, lost two head of cattle. . . . Two more nights with my saddle for a pillow and I will be home once more.[44]

While escort duty was popular with the men, the commanders through their messages had other opinions especially when troop strength was low. Captain Tilford, 3rd Cavalry, trying to offset the lack of manpower by having men from other posts meet his escorts halfway was told by headquarters, "your escorts will go as far as McRae."[45] They also disliked the fact that the men were out of their immediate control, and the court-martial records showed there were some good reasons for that. In June 1868 Private James Freeman, Troop K, 3rd Cavalry, absented himself from an escort party for a drink while the party passed through Leasburg. He was found guilty of being AWOL and fined twelve dollars. The records did not show whether the party was just starting out or on their way back to Fort Selden.

After 1867 the district commander assigned escort missions by priority because of the low strength of the command. The district restricted Fort Selden's efforts primarily to high-ranking government officials according to the following messages that were sent in 1868:

> . . . Governor Mitchell is to visit. Insure he receives honors due his position and suitable escort.
> . . . Furnish escort for the U.S. Marshal of El Paso to Fort Craig.
> . . . Provide suitable escort for the Honorable J. Houghton, US District Judge of Mesilla.
> . . . Provide every courtesy to Bishop Lamy
> . . . Provide escort for Chief Justice J. G. Palen to Fort Cummings and return.
> . . . Provide suitable escort and every facility for the wife of Judge Knapp of Las Cruces to Santa Fe[46]

Lieutenant Colonel Devin, 8th Cavalry, received instructions to receive the governor coming down during the raids of 1871. "His Excellency, William A. Pile, the Governor of the Territory is to visit scenes of recent Indian raids. You will provide him with every assistance and escort."[47]

As the troubles with Victorio and the Ojo Caliente Apaches ended so did the need for escort. Messages of the late 1870s and early 1880s indicated that wagon trains and stages were leaving Las Cruces and Fort Selden with no escort at all. In April 1877 Captain Carroll, 9th Cavalry, sent a six-mule team and wagon with a private in charge to Fort Stanton without the benefit of an escort.[48] After 1881 there were no messages referencing escort duty in the post's records.

## Communications

Another form of military operations that contributed to the development of the southern region was the establishment of a military communication system. With the advent of the telegraph this was usually done by a separate command called the Signal Corps, but in the early years each command established its own. Communication was the glue that held the forts and operations together, though at times the various communication systems seemed more destined to disrupt than assist. Fort Selden used many forms of communication. The early means were limited to express riders, stagecoaches, and military wagon trains. Later, post communications were improved and expanded to include the telegraph, heliograph, and finally the railroad system.

The communications systems to support combat operations in the field and to transmit orders and reports between the Fort Selden and its various headquarters were slow and cumbersome. The quickest method for sending reports before the telegraph was by express riders, but they were subject to interception by hostile Apaches or bandits, who primarily wanted their horses and equipment. In 1863 the bodies of two express riders were found between Fort Craig and Santa Fe. The mail with $115 in currency was strewn over a large area, but the only items missing were the rider's clothes and horses.[49] In July 1871 the *New Mexican* reported that Apaches had killed the express mail rider from La Mesilla to Tucson and stole his horse and weapon.[50]

While the express riders provided the quickest form of communication, it still took several days for the messages to reach Santa Fe. Captain Wilbur F. DuBois, 15th Infantry, requested permission by express rider to hire a guide for his movement to Arizona on 15 February 1870. The district message granting permission arrived at Fort Selden on 3 March 1870, but DuBois and his company had departed on 25 February.[51] Another commander, in response to a district request for a soldier to come to Santa Fe, stated that the soldier was on extended patrol and even with an express rider the man could not be in Santa Fe by the time requested.[52]

Another factor that slowed communications was the availability of grog shops and saloons along the routes as express riders sometimes succumbed to the evils of alcohol. There were several instances in the court-martial records of dispatch riders being charged with drunkenness and failure to do their duty.

Routine messages were sent through the regular mail service, either by the scheduled stagecoach or by buckboard. Fort Selden usually had two stagecoaches come through in a week, unless bad weather had closed the road to Santa Fe. Rain, running arroyos, swollen rivers, snow and other forms of bad weather slowed the mail. In June 1881 the *Rio Grande Republican* reported that Fort Selden had both a post office and a postmaster, but had received no mail due to transportation difficulties with weather.

The first post office at Fort Selden was established in 1865 and was an "on and off" operation for the life of the fort. Many times it was located in the post trader's store. This caused the post commander some problems. Illegal liquor by the bottle sales to the soldiers forced Captain Charles Hulhammer, 15th Infantry, to close the trader's store temporarily in October 1876. The postmaster sided with the post trader in the argument and refused to deliver the mail. Hulhammer wrote to headquarters in Santa Fe, "The postmaster has refused to receive or deliver the mail because I closed the trader's store. . . .This may affect my ability to comply promptly with orders."[53] This problem was smoothed over, but in 1877 the postmaster resigned, and the mail was delivered sporadically from Doña Ana, a town about eight miles south of Fort Selden.

In 1878 Lieutenant William Cory, 15th Infantry, complained to the Postmaster General:

Mail arrives from Aleman Station and Doña Ana on Mondays and Thursdays by stage coach . . . the mail from Aleman's is expeditious, but the mail from Doña Ana sometimes is not taken from the stage . . . goes all the way to Aleman and then returns. . . . sometimes late in compliance to orders . . . respectfully request all mail go to Las

Cruces for bagging then by buckboard to Fort Selden.[54]

Las Cruces, as requested, was then designated as the post office for Fort Selden, and the mail forwarded to the post by buckboard. However, this arrangement proved no more expeditious than Doña Ana. On 5 July 1878 Cory complained to the postmistress in Las Cruces, "the mail that was to be delivered by buckboard did not arrive." Fort Selden's problems with mail delivery were not solved until the arrival of the railroad in 1881. However, a new communication system arrived in 1876 that excited the Mesilla Valley and alleviated many of the time lag problems suffered by the military.

The military telegraph system had an immediate effect on the number of messages sent and on the efficiency of the post's communications. The telegraph lines reached Fort Selden in March 1876. The post return for March reported: "The wires reached this post on the 18th." Fort Selden had averaged eight messages a month to higher headquarters prior to the arrival of the telegraph, but with the wires now linking the post to headquarters, as many as eight messages were sent in one day.

The telegraph also had its own set of problems causing delays and missed deadlines. Breaks in the lines would delay orders, for example, and commanders would have to send valuable manpower to protect the repairmen. On 4 August 1876, someone cut the wire in Cooke's Canyon stopping all messages to the west and slowing vital messages during the start of Victorio's War. In another incident the wire was stolen between Las Cruces and Engle (located about eight miles east of present day Truth or Consequences on the Jornada del Muerto); then flash floods washed away the poles. Both of these episodes eliminated communications to the north for several weeks. Captain Henry Carroll, 9th Cavalry, highlighted the problem of downed lines when he did not respond to a requested district mission. He explained on 29 April 1876, "Your telegram dated 14 April was just received."[55]

The telegraphic messages became rather terse and cryptic when compared to the formerly written messages. For example, on

30 June 1876, the following report was sent to Santa Fe: "Forty four (44) serviceable, one (1) lost, drowned, today eleven (11) temporarily unserviceable, one (1) left at Tularosa." The subject was omitted, but this was probably a status report on mules or horses, not soldiers or weapons. The receiver and the sender knew because there was no follow-up message.

When Fort Selden was abandoned in 1878, the military telegraph office moved to La Mesilla providing a needed service to that town. On reoccupation of the post in 1881 Captain Gustavus M. Bascom, 13th Infantry, reestablished the post's telegraph office and rewired the post into both Las Cruces and La Mesilla providing instant communication with both towns. His system did not last though. Western Union took over the military telegraph line between Las Cruces and the post on 2 May 1882, and on 31 May 1882, closed the office at Fort Selden. Fort Selden was again without direct communication service, but the military telegraph office in La Mesilla continued to function. The post commander was angry when Fort Selden without a telegraph office was ordered to send a soldier to assist the military office in La Mesilla.[56] The United States Army Signal Department, responsible for the installation and maintenance of the military telegraph system, seemed to have decided to close Fort Selden before the War Department did.

The military telegraph line appeared on some messages faster or more efficient than the Western Union line. The *Rio Grande Republican* complained in its 9 July 1881 issue, "the news of the shooting of President James Garfield arrived from Western Union at 8 AM on Sunday, but the military telegraph in La Mesilla had received the news at 12 AM on Saturday some 21 hours earlier."

Even with the loss of the telegraph office at Fort Selden, communications had improved since 1865. Direct mail service had been established with the arrival of the railroad in 1881, and two trains arrived daily. So even though the post had lost the telegraph and outgoing communications were back to written messages for a short time, the system was still faster and more reliable than the stagecoach or dispatch rider. At times the district and the department headquarters sent telegrams, but these messages had to go to La Mesilla (military telegraph station) or Las Cruces (Western Union) and then be relayed by buckboard or by train to Fort Selden, which made them not much faster than messages by train direct. Captain MacArthur, 13th Infantry, wrote the superintendent of Western Union about the poor service: "A telegram from Las Cruces was not sent to Fort Selden, but was thrown off a passing train . . . only by good fortune was it picked up by a post officer."[57] With permission from the area railroad supervisor, MacArthur in 1866, with his flair for getting things done, connected into the telegraph line at Rincon, a switching station for the AT&SF railroad about 10 miles north of Fort Selden. MacArthur provided his own operator and reported to the department headquarters in Arizona. "I have a moderately good operator who runs the telegraph office at this post . . . and another soldier who understands Morse, but has no experience as an operator."[58]

The last communications system installed at the post was to assist the commander of the post or district in communicating directly with the troops in the field. The railroad and telegraph had brought rapid communications between posts and headquarters, but the express rider was still the only method between the post and the patrol. Major General Nelson Miles, who had relieved Major General George Crook as commander of the Department of Arizona, established heliograph detachments consisting of two or three men on peaks across southern Arizona and New Mexico.

A heliograph was a shuttered mirror on a tripod. Through manipulation of the shutter the operator sent flashes of sunlight in Morse code to the next station. Each post was assigned a heliograph and an "area of observation."[59] The station at Fort Selden was placed on a peak in the Robledo mountains (now referred to as Signal Peak by the locals, but Lookout Peak by the map makers), which afforded the post communication in several directions; west via Cooke's Peak to Arizona, south with Fort Bliss via Mount Franklin, and east with Fort Stanton direct.[60] The only reported use of the heliograph at Fort Selden was in 1888 when Lieutenant James E. Brett reported to the district that he had communicated with his patrol in the San Andres Mountains with the system.[61]

In summary, the communications between Fort Selden and its headquarters and between Fort Selden and its field operations continued to be a problem throughout the post's life. MacArthur's 1886 report showed a vast change in the forms of communication since the post's inception in May 1865. The post now had a post office, telegraph office, daily mail deliveries by rail both north and south, and the blinking light of the heliograph.[62] But Fort Selden's commanders still received information and orders late, and were forced to make decisions and commit troops based on their best judgment without waiting for approval from headquarters. In numerous instances the commander taking action ended up in trouble with his headquarters, when the action taken was deemed not acceptable. Yet, had the commander waited to get permission, the fleeting chance to act would have disappeared. An example was Lieutenant Colonel Thomas C. Devin's rapid response (discussed in more detail in Chapter 5) with troops to a political confrontation in La Mesilla in 1871. When the District Headquarters at Santa Fe was informed, their reaction was: "By whose authority did you commit troops to Mesilla?" Santa Fe seemed to be more worried usurping civilian authority than preventing mayhem in La Mesilla, yet Devin's rapid reaction undoubtedly saved lives and possibly prevented a small war such as later occurred in Lincoln County.[63]

**Day-to-Day Operations**

Historian Don Rickey described the western post's daily operations as, "extremely monotonous . . . and a rather dull existence."[64] Fort Selden was no different. The men woke to the bugle, ate by the bugle, went to work by the bugle, and were put to bed by the bugle, except for the previously mentioned period when the bugler, Jacob Bath, had lost his teeth. Reveille was sounded at sunrise and taps at 8:30 PM., and even the first sergeant working in the company orderly room had to have the commander's permission to keep his lights on past taps. The commander in 1883 grudgingly gave permission to the first sergeant of Troop B, 4th Cavalry, who was preparing reports to have a light until 10:00 PM.[65]

Work or fatigue details included cleaning the corrals, tending the post's gardens, repair work on the buildings, police call, cleaning the "sinks" (latrines), cleaning the barracks, and kitchen police. Not a lot of excitement is to be found in those details. The worst of the work detail had to have been guard duty.

The soldiers selected for guard duty were assigned from a roster kept by the first sergeant. Every man on the post was required to stand guard at one time or another, except those with special duties such as hospital orderly, cook, or company clerk. The guard force at Fort Selden was posted in the morning and remained on duty for a twenty-four hour period. The guard mount, as it was called, was a formation of only those soldiers selected for the next twenty-four hours. It included an inspection of the guard's uniform and equipment by the officer-of-the-day, and the soldiers had to recite the special orders for their particular guard post. Several soldiers received court-martials for failing to remember the special orders of their particular post.[66]

Guards were actually on duty for two hours and off for four during the twenty-four hour period of their duty. During the four hours of off duty time they had to remain available in the guardhouse, and were responsible to oversee the prisoners doing hard labor. The two hours on duty meant walking their post and challenging anyone approaching. Several men were court-martialed for sitting down during the duty, or improper challenges. The duty at times could be most unpleasant due to the cold, rain, or sandstorms, but night duty had to be especially bad. Coyote calls, skunks, and moonless nights added to the sometimes-inclement weather, made an uncomfortable night for the guard. The worst duty must have been guarding the post cattle herd. The herd was usually away from the cantonment area grazing, so the guard faced not only the inclement weather and loneliness, but also the likelihood of dangerous raids.

All of the guards were required to be in full dress uniform or blues, which were heavy wool uniforms. That uniform would be fine for the winter months, but must have been terrible in the summer. Many soldiers must have either collapsed from heat exhaustion or reported in sick while on guard duty. The post surgeon in 1874 made a strong recommendation to the post commander. "It is decidedly too hot for the men to wear full dress. . . . Recommend that officers and men mount guard in undress."[67] Undress was removal of the heavy blouse, but the wool pants remained.

Another boring detail was post clean up, referred to as police call in the modern military. This detail usually occurred immediately after breakfast and before work call. The effort or lack of effort, of the detail upset the surgeon because there was a comment on the men's poor sanitation almost monthly in his report to headquarters. In his report for December 1874, he stated that, the yards and root cellars needed "policing."[68] In the February 1875 report, the surgeon complained that the stagecoach company area needed "police badly," and their employees had thrown "dung out of the corral onto the post road."[69] In January 1876, the inspector pointed out that the detail cleaning the sinks and latrines had done a poor job, and the kitchen police, Private Wilson, "did not do his duty for the dishes and bowls were filthy."[70]

When the monthly report did not get the desired results the surgeon would submit a formal letter to the commander. In January 1876, the surgeon complained to the post adjutant in a formal letter, "the men are doing a poor job of police, there is rusty bed frame in back of the barracks that has been there for two months."[71]

More strong evidence that the troops did not care for clean up detail is found in the garrison court-martial records. Through the years several men were charged with "failure to obey a lawful order" when directed to go on police call. On 14 September 1869 a saddler, Thomas Roache, refused to police his yard and received a stiff sentence of seven days at hard labor and a fifteen-dollar fine.[72] However, even with all the complaints by the Post Surgeon and the punishment dished out by the court-martial boards, the post always got favorable press. The local papers and visitors always commented favorably on the post and its neat and clean appearance.

## Training

Another post detail was military training for new recruits and retraining for old soldiers. There is some evidence that the soldiers at Fort Selden received marksmanship, mounted and dismounted drill, and signals training at least monthly. Drills, such as the manual of arms, facing movements, and horsemanship, were scheduled twice daily as part of the post's routine, but it is unclear if the training was actually conducted because manpower always seemed to be in short supply. Other specialized training, such as; the making and carrying by field stretchers, tactics, signals, and instruction on army regulations, seems to have occurred only when directed by the district commander. Signals instruction included semaphore, writing messages, and later practice with Morse code.

As early as September 1871, the post commander, Lieutenant Colonel Devin, 8th Cavalry, reported that the men had received instruction in military signals.[73] Signals instruction was to be monthly, but at times the officers at Fort Selden either forgot or had no one available to teach. In May 1872 district headquarters wanted a detailed explanation as to "why" Fort Selden had had no signals instruction.[74]

The troops were also required to do target practice. On 8 June 1875 the post commander reminded the commander of Troop A, 8th Cavalry, "I have not yet received your May report of target shooting."[75] In October 1883 Captain P. H. Ellis, 13th Infantry, responded to a request from Santa Fe as to the status of Fort Selden's marksmanship range.

The rifle range is of standard distances . . . with an abutment of 8 feet filled with dirt at the end. The targets face south. . . . 20 rounds allotted per man per month. Cavalry uses the Hotchkiss carbine and the Infantry has Springfield rifle (45 caliber).[76]

Safety requirements during rifle practice on the range must not have been a primary concern. The surgeon complained in June 1876, that the rounds from target practice, "especially those of Troop F, 9th

Cavalry," were going across the road used by travelers and toward the ferry into the clumps of cottonwoods frequented by cattle.[77]

Other training demanded by headquarters, included instruction in army regulations, and training in making field expedient stretchers. Captain Gregory Barrett, 10th Infantry, reported, "Theoretical instruction in army regulations has been given to officers . . . but the enlisted men are constantly at work cleaning the post and putting it in the proper condition."[78] The surgeon was pleased with his training efforts in 1888. He reported on the training in the construction of expedient stretchers, such as blankets wrapped around two rifles, or poles with blankets pulled behind a mule, that in each case: "The patient was moved some distance with ease and comfort."[79]

However, the primary method of instruction at Fort Selden for the new recruit and reassigned soldiers was what the army now refers to as on-the-job training or OJT. Each newly arrived man was assigned to an "old hand," and his "bunkie" or bunkmate was then responsible for his "upbringing." Quick learning meant survival. The cavalry fought as mounted infantry; they rode the horse to battle, but then dismounted and fought on foot. The newly reassigned man or recruit was usually responsible for holding the squad's horses until he learned the tactics, or until the squad had confidence in him.

This brief synopsis of the efforts put forth by the officers and men of Fort Selden cannot do them justice. The conduct of military operations through many hardships and problems brought about the pacification of southern New Mexico. Through the field operations, such as the patrol, outpost and reactive operations, the soldiers provided security to ranchers, government agents, merchants moving goods, travelers, mail, settlers and citizens. The efforts to establish reliable communications aided not only the post but the local citizenry as well. Finally, those military operations much less heroic than the dashing about the countryside chasing hostiles, such as post details and training efforts supported the soldiers and produced units capable of accomplishing their varied missions.

**Army Spring Wagon**

# 4

# Logistics

Logistics is the branch of military science that includes the procurement, maintenance, and transportation of men, materiel, and animals. This aspect of the post's operations, especially the purchase of local goods and services, was the most important economic element of the interactions between post and local settlements. Because of the distance to the usual eastern supply points and the high cost of freight, the southwestern posts were required to procure food, fuel (wood, charcoal, and coal), hay and other forage, building materials, transportation, and labor locally.

The War Department made those local purchases contingent on competitive pricing. The policies were promulgated throughout the region via the Santa Fe *New Mexican* in its 4 September 1871 edition.

> Advertising for supplies or forage shall be open to settlers, farmers and stock raisers. No award will be made until local proposals are received and compared with those [from the states] received at headquarters. . . . It is proper to give the neighboring settlers a market for their produce providing that they are willing to sell at a price competitive with produce that can be brought from a distance.

There is evidence that the merchants of the Mesilla Valley made good use of this policy. The quartermaster records and letters indicate a considerable amount of cash was funneled into the settlements around Fort Selden prior to the arrival of the railroad. After 1881 the availability of rapid transport via the railroads turned the focus of Fort Selden's logistical system away from local procurement and toward Fort Leavenworth, Kansas.

Probably the most important logistical function was feeding the soldiers and stock. Sun Tzu, a Chinese general, wrote some 2,500 years ago:

> When an army feeds its horses with grain and kills its cattle for food, and when the men do not hang their cooking pots over campfires, showing they will not return to their tents, you may know that they are determined to fight to the death.[1]

This observation certainly applied to the men of Fort Selden during patrol operations. Their horses were carefully fed with grain, their cattle were killed as a basic food source, the soldiers stayed away from their barracks, they slept on the ground rolled in blankets, and they ate many meals without the benefit of fires.

**Feeding Fort Selden's Soldiers**

The trooper's patrol rations were extremely simple. Hardtack or the army biscuit accompanied by salted beef or pork was the mainstay. Most of the time, the rations had to be eaten on the move or during the short breaks and without fires. But when the evening rest stop allowed fires, the fry pan was brought out and a hot meal was prepared, each individual cooking to his own taste. This is a patrol meal as described by a private. "Hardtack was soaked in water if available then fried in grease, after the pork. Brown sugar was sprinkled over . . . not a bad meal."[2]

Each man carried three-quarters of a pound of meat, a pound of hardtack, and coffee as a day's ration, plus corn and grain for his horse.

This amount of food and weight necessitated that the patrol either be followed by a supply wagon or make some other arrangements for re-supply. There were times at Fort Selden when the commander had trouble getting enough rations to supply his patrols.

Major Lane, 3rd Cavalry, complained to the district commissary officer that he had insufficient bacon on hand to support a large operation in 1869. He had ordered 9,500 pounds of bacon, which had not arrived. The shortage forced him to borrow from Forts Cummings and Craig, and he still had to borrow an additional 775 pounds of bacon from a Las Cruces citizen. This shortage delayed the start of the operation by one day.[3] It is difficult to ascertain whether this particular problem arose because of poor planning on Lane's part, or the transportation system. The delivery time of this shipment of bacon took more than fifty days from Fort Union to Fort Selden a distance of approximately 300 miles.[4] The usual procedure was to plan far enough in advance to insure sufficient rations and equipment on hand prior to the start of the operation. To expect the supply system to produce 9,500 pounds of bacon rapidly seems to have been wishful thinking.

There were other examples of shortages. In May 1872, Major David R. Clendenin, 8th Cavalry, reported to the chief quartermaster officer in Santa Fe, "You failed to send us flour and we have none." A lack of flour would have made it difficult to bake bread or biscuits, the staples of the Fort Selden company mess halls. Clendenin also had to borrow 500 pounds of coffee in 1872 from a Las Cruces merchant to insure sufficient coffee for his post and patrol needs; he had also requested permission to buy coffee locally at 36 cents a pound. The tenor of the messages between headquarters and Fort Selden on the amount of coffee Clendenin had borrowed indicated the district quartermaster officer thought that he was doing something with the coffee other than brewing drinks for the troops.[5] Clendenin responded quite tersely to the quartermaster in Santa Fe on 29 May 1872:

The coffee (1000 pounds) transferred from Fort Cummings received at Fort Selden on April 19. 500 lbs. were used to pay back the post trader. Quartermaster ought to keep himself informed of wants of different posts. When I was in Santa Fe I told the QM I had received the 1000 lbs., but due to pay back would be out by 1 June. . . .

Clendenin did not receive an apology for the innuendo, but did receive "coffee and other stores" by the middle of June.

The food served to the soldiers while at the post was somewhat more diverse than the patrol rations, but there was no indication that it was any better. In fact, the number of garrison court-martials resulting from thrown food in the mess hall, together with the complaints about both the quality and quantity of food, indicated that the troopers were not always pleased with the cook's efforts.

As mentioned in Chapter 1, each company or troop had its own mess hall and kitchen. The cook was either a volunteer or a detailed soldier and had received no special training from the army on the culinary arts. He cooked on a sheet iron stove fueled with charcoal or wood. The typical menu included meat, potatoes or beans, bread, and coffee. Sometimes the meal was supplemented with fresh vegetables from the company garden and canned goods such as peaches, cranberry sauce, and tomatoes. There is no evidence to show that they augmented their daily menu with the common food of the region such as burritos, tacos, enchiladas, or tamales, but it can be assumed that this was the case when the patrol or soldier came into contact with the local ranches or communities.

The post's baker provided the bread served by the mess halls. Each man while in garrison was authorized eighteen ounces of bread, or flour a day. At times the flour ration was increased to offset losses in other foodstuffs. In October 1875, the post surgeon asked that the ration be raised to twenty-two ounces a day because the supplemental crackers "were moldy, wormy, and unfit for man's use."[6]

The ovens used to bake the bread were of mud, built by local labor, and were preferred by some of the commanders and bakers over the army issued camp stove.[7] Captain Gustavus Bascom, 13th Infantry, refused an offer from the quartermaster in Santa Fe in July 1882 to replace his ovens. "Thank you for offering the use of the portable field ovens, but we are using an excellent adobe oven."[8] Captain Gregory Barrett, 10th Infantry, also turned down the ovens in 1886. "My baker has found a bake house and is now using it to bake bread."[9] Barrett did not say where he had found it, but since they are not moveable, it was probably in the same place it had been since 1865. The editor of the Santa Fe *New Mexican* was not as thrilled as the Seldenites over the mud ovens:

> The government bakery [at Fort Marcy, District Headquarters in Santa Fe] has a fine brick and stone oven with a brick chimney. It is the only one like it in the territory. . . . All others are constructed of mud in the shape of a Musquaque hat.[10]

The flour to bake Fort Selden's bread came from local sources until the arrival of the railroad. Historian Darlis Miller stated that the army's need for flour is what started the neophyte milling business in the Southwest, but with the arrival of the railroad the small mills disappeared after a few years.[11] Fort Selden's need for bread created a local wheat and flour market for the merchants of Las Cruces, La Mesilla, and Socorro. In fact the post at times tended to buy more than could be used resulting in loss to mildew and weevils. In March 1873 Major Clendenin, 8th Cavalry, complained that the commissary officer had let a contract to Henry Lesinsky of Las Cruces for 80,000 pounds of flour, while the post still had 59,363 pounds on hand. "The storage of new flour is a waste to worms and mice. . . . And a new storehouse will have to be built. . . . I respectfully protest the purchase of flour."[12]

There were many and varied complaints about the local flour, primarily centered on the amount of grit and overall quality. Major Lane, 3rd Cavalry, in 1869 stated that the flour received from "Emmanuel Vehil" [Manuel Vigil of Socorro] was not of the quality of that shipped from the east. He also instructed his commissary officer to do a better job of inspecting the goods, "The flour must meet contract standards.

. . . If you are not a judge of good flour you must have some baked to test it. . . . It has been officially complained of as sandy."[13]

The identity of the "official" complainer was not revealed, but Lane's wife was certainly a likely candidate. The wheat used to create the "sandy" flour was also grown locally. The Mesilla Valley *Independent* in 1877 stated that the wheat crops gave great promise of exceeding any previous harvest and would probably bring $2.50 a fanega."[14]

Another local purchase that impacted on the local economy was meat. Beef for the soldiers was purchased locally between 1865 and 1891; the only change in supplying beef for the post was the manner of delivery after 1881. The post purchased cattle, and had its own herd from 1865–1881. This necessitated hiring herders, and a Fort Selden officer, usually the officer of the day, was assigned the additional duty of overseeing the herd. In 1881 it was Second Lieutenant Mitchell's responsibility. He was chastised by the post commander after the disappearance of some of the beef. "You will in the future cause the post herd to be grazed within the immediate vicinity of this post. You will make one visit daily to see if the herders are in saddles as ordered."[15]

Each month Fort Selden reported to Santa Fe on the status of its herd, and as would be expected the reports varied from bad to glowing. On 21 June 1871 Lieutenant Colonel Thomas C. Devin, 8th Cavalry, wrote to his commissary officer at Fort Selden. "The men complain of the quality of meat. . . . You are directed to take steps authorized by the terms and stipulations of the contract to insure healthy beef in the command."[16] A report to headquarters in October 1875 indicated, ". . . . Small number of men therefore less demand on the beef herd. They are in first class condition. . . . Good forage this year."[17] The surgeon the same year indicated even if the beef was good, to eat it three times and day and seven days a week was wearisome, "The food is well cooked. . . . The beef is monotonous recommend that bacon and beans be substituted at least twice weekly."[18]

After the post was reoccupied in 1881, meat was still procured locally. However the unit strength was so low that butchered meat rather than on-the-hoof beef was purchased. There were numerous problems with both delivery and quality. In May 1884 Captain Arthur MacArthur, 13th Infantry, complained to headquarters, "The small number of men makes it exceedingly difficult to supply the command with good beef, unless the contractor has an agent on post with 'contrivances' and ice."[19] The next month he requested permission to issue salt meat during the hot months because, "The meat provided by contractor from El Paso comes by refrigerated car, but there is no way to store it at Fort Selden."[20]

The delivery by rail and refrigerated car was a great improvement but still left room for stupidity. In May 1889 Lieutenant James Brett, 24th Infantry, sent this message to his supplier in El Paso, "The meat was thrown off the train in an outrageous manner and rolled about 50 feet."[21] That incident and the territorial legislature passing a bill prohibiting the shipment of fresh meat across the New Mexico border, led to a new contract with A. G. Smith, a butcher in Las Cruces, which remained in effect until the post closed in 1891.[22]

Beef was sometimes replaced with wild game or fish. The post surgeon in 1885 reported to Washington: "Antelope and deer are occasionally shot on the reservation and quail and dove are numerous enough to insure a full bag to a good shot."[23] And again in 1889 he reported that, "The men were not issued fresh beef today. . . . They took fish from the river."[24]

Another mainstay for the soldiers was bacon, especially for patrol duty. Some bacon was purchased locally from George Clark in San Augustine (now known as Organ), a small mining community twenty miles east of Las Cruces, for a short time between 1868–1870, but most of the bacon came from the east.[25] The long trek did not do it any good. In 1870 Major Clendenin, 8th Cavalry, instructed the commissary officer to, "Send no more rotten bacon. . . . Provide [for] local purchase instead."[26] The storage of bacon in the hot weather also posed a problem for the fort. The surgeon in his monthly inspection in April 1876 informed the commander, "You must use drip troughs to catch the melting drip from the bacon in the storeroom."[27] The spring heat was cooking the bacon and the dripping grease was causing a fly problem.

The beans that the surgeon wanted to substitute for the "monotonous" beef were primarily a subsistence crop in the Mesilla Valley. With an increased demand from the army, small farmers began growing beans as a cash crop.[28] Requests for proposals of beans appeared almost monthly in the Santa Fe *New Mexican*. An army advertisement in the newspaper in January 1868 called for "6,000 pounds of beans, dried, full and smooth in good strong sacks."[29] The post must have had some problems with the beans delivered from Louis Rosenbaum in 1874. The post trader, A.H. Moorehead, was appointed a disinterested person for the government and Adolphe Lea was the agent for Rosenbaum to look into the "case of bad beans."[30] The result of this investigation was not included in the letters sent files.

Vegetables were usually available either through local purchase, the commissary officer, or the company's gardens. Post records do not reveal the type of vegetables grown at Fort Selden, but the local press indicated that tomatoes, onions, cabbage, beets, parsnips, carrots, turnips, and potatoes were part of a bumper crop in the Mesilla Valley in 1871. Fresh fruit was also available locally. The *La Mesilla News* stated in May 1874, that La Mesilla and Doña Ana had a tremendous crop of pears, apples, grapes, strawberries, pecans, and peaches.[32] The local fruit found its way to the soldiers' diet. In his monthly report of August 1885 the surgeon stated that the men had, "an occasional case of diarrhea or colic from eating large quantities of ripe and green fruit."[32]

Each company had its own garden, and a well was dug to provide a ready access to water. The quartermaster provided the seed. The gardens were not always successful, nor were they popular as a detail with the men, but their importance in preventing scurvy was well known by the surgeon and officers.

So important were the vegetables to Captain Phillip H. Ellis, 13th Infantry, stationed at Fort Bayard in 1883 that he wanted to send men to raise a garden before his unit was assigned to Fort Selden. "If I am to be sent to Selden request permission to send two men now to prepare a company garden."[33] The gardens were not as important to others. In June 1875 the surgeon reported that Company J, 15th Infantry, had plenty of vegetables but the diet of Troop H, 8th Cavalry, was "seriously lacking" because "their garden had been destroyed by a soldier who has since gone without leave."[34] The district policy of rotating troops also affected their gardening. In February 1871, the two troops at Fort Selden that had gardens were scheduled to move to Fort Stanton on a normal rotation. Lieutenant Colonel Devin, 8th Cavalry, requested that the incoming troops send men ahead "to tend to the gardens" so as not to lose all the work put in by Troops F and G.[35]

The capricious desert weather also played a big part in the availability of vegetables. In October 1875 Lieutenant Casper A. Conrad, 15th Infantry, asked for help from Santa Fe as there had been a complete failure of his company's garden due to excessive rain. In June 1887 Captain Gregory Barrett, 10th Infantry, sent a special request for vegetables to the district commissary officer because rain and hail had destroyed his unit's garden crop.

Potatoes, though grown in the valley, were shipped in from the states, and in the 1870s Fort Selden seemed to have been the southern distribution point of potatoes for the district. In December 1871 Major Clendenin, 8th Cavalry, wrote to the commander at Fort Bayard: "Potatoes arrived at this post. . . . Your pro rata share will be sent, but no transportation at this time."[36] In December 1876 Captain Carroll, 9th Cavalry, notified Fort Craig that "potatoes have arrived but are frostbitten. . . . Send wagon for your share."[37]

Shortages of potatoes like other rations caused irate messages to flow. Lieutenant James Brett, 24th Infantry, commanding the post in 1889, demanded to know when he was to receive his potatoes as the post had "been out of potatoes and onions for four months." When Brett received the potatoes another irate message, "Out of the 23 bags of potatoes shipped we received only 20." And finally in November a brief comment back to Fort Bayard, "received 800 lbs of potatoes"[38]

With the arrival of the railroad in 1881 the diet of the soldier at Fort Selden changed somewhat. Beef and bread were still the primary diet, but the trains from Fort Leavenworth now brought codfish, dried fruit, and all kinds of canned goods, including cranberry sauce, oatmeal, jams, and canned milk.[39] Supply had finally caught up with the demand.

## The Quest for Water

If the railroad brought more and better foodstuffs, the water system remained the same throughout most of the life of the fort. Captain MacArthur, 13th Infantry, in his 1886 report to the Division of the Pacific stated, "The water is still hauled from the river each day by mule team and water wagon."[40] There is no evidence that a well was ever dug at the company kitchens or quarters of the post, but a well was dug at the gardens on the reservation. In August 1889, the surgeon reported:

> The river is slow flowing, stagnant and unwholesome . . . stomach and intestinal troubles are appearing. . . . The old well at the garden has been cleared out and sunk a few feet deeper to about 10 1/2 feet. . . .It is clearer than the river water. . . . Recommend a driven well.[41]

His recommendation must have been taken, for the monthly sanitation report of September 1889 stated, "The post now has a driven well to the depth of 24 feet and the water is excellent." A "driven" well indicated that they used pipe driven down to the water table, but this well's location has been lost.

General Douglas MacArthur, son of the post commander Arthur MacArthur, remembered the fun and excitement of the "bumpy rides on the mule drawn water wagon that would make the daily trip to the Rio Grande."[42] The daily trip to the Rio Grande for water may have provided entertainment for the children of the post, but the quality of the water brought back to the post was suspect. Lydia Spencer Lane provided an insight on water quality:

> Water was brought fresh every morning from the muddy Rio Grande. The water was the color of rich chocolate. . . . It was

poured into large earthen jars . . . by degrees the impurities sank to the bottom of the jar, then water oozed through [the clay sides of the olla] keeping the contents quite cool.[43]

The daily water gathering procedure was fairly simple, but required man power, mule power and time. There is no record showing who was charged with the responsibility of filling all the water barrels on post, whether it was the cooks, the officer of the day, the quartermaster, or a regular detail of the guard mount. In any case, the water wagon or tank was driven into the river, filled with water by hand using buckets, and pulled back to the post. Then the detail filled each of the water barrels and ollas (large porous clay pots) outside the quarters, barracks, kitchens, laundry, and hospital. The result of this time-consuming effort was muddy brown water for drinking, washing, and cooking.

In 1876, the surgeon recommended to the post commander, "Since the river was rising and would be filled with impurities. . . . Treat with permanganate of potassium to clear."[44] In June of the same year he remarked, "If you let the water stand for 8-12 hours it becomes tolerably clean."[45] It seems that a more appropriate word would have been "tolerably" clear not clean, since clean suggests safe to drink.

The water barrels and ollas must have accumulated interesting mosses, algae, and other organisms from the river. The various surgeons' reports over the years 1876–1890 indicated that the soldiers were not cleaning the barrels, as they should have. The comment "the water barrels must be cleaned each time before refilling" appeared frequently in the Monthly Sanitation Reports. However, there was never a suggestion from the surgeon to boil the river water to assist with purification.

**Fuel**

Fuel was needed to cook and to warm the barracks and quarters. The primary fuels used at Fort Selden were mesquite root, charcoal, and coal, and all were purchased locally.

The mesquite root presented a unique problem in that its gnarled and twisted roots would not allow the wood to lie flat, so that stacking for purchase by the cord was difficult. In 1869 Major Lane, 3rd Cavalry, asked district headquarters how to measure a cord of mesquite root:

> As you know if the crooked roots are badly put up without being cut or care taken . . . a half cord can be made to measure a cord. . . . Recommend this phrase be put in the contract . . . the mesquite shafts be cut and stacked for measurement so that no more space will be left in a quantity of wood than would ordinarily occur.[46]

This system must not have worked or else it was not passed on to other commanders, because the problem continued. In 1881 Captain Gustavus Bascom, 13th Infantry, told his post quartermaster that it was impossible to pile mesquite root, "therefore, issue as received as 9 feet per cord."[47]

Fuel in the desert was expensive. In August 1875, Louis Rosenbaum of Las Cruces provided 500 cords of mesquite root at $6.35 a cord.[48] This compared unfavorably to wood at Fort Stanton costing $3 a cord but cheap compared to Fort Cummings wood, which cost $15.50 a cord.[49] The army's need to economize determined which type of fuel, wood, charcoal, or coal, would be used at Fort Selden during a particular year.

In 1869, Major Lane, 3rd Cavalry, was using mesquite to heat and cook, but by the early 1870s the commanders were using charcoal. H.C. Herring of Las Cruces obtained the charcoal contract in 1875 providing 1,500 bushels of charcoal at forty-three cents a bushel. Then in the late 1870s and early 1880s coal was purchased from Los Cerillos Mine near Santa Fe and freighted to Fort Selden. The post had on hand 7,800 pounds of coal in 1881.[50] No matter which fuel was used in a particular year, it burned up a major portion of the post's annual budget.

## Equipment

Another area of concern in logistics was the men's equipment. The equipment issued to the soldiers was not designed for arid or semi-arid terrain, nor did there ever seem to be enough. The wool uniform was too heavy in summer and too light in high country during the winter. Shortages of powder, weapons, and clothing hampered operations throughout the life of the post.

In May 1868 Captain Tilford, 3rd Cavalry, reported to the district that the post was, "out of powder cannot fire the daily salute." The post had a 12 pound and a 6 pound cannon for this purpose. Not only was the post missing powder it was also missing individual weapons. The Inspector General in 1866 reported that one-fourth of the troops at Fort Selden did not have weapons. The lack of weapons was shocking, but it is more understandable after reading a message from district headquarters dated 25 September, "It has been reported that troops from Company K, 38th Infantry, are selling their uniforms and equipment including weapons. What are you doing about it?"[52] Since Tilford himself was accused of selling arms, and was relieved of command for it, it is doubtful that anything was done.

Weapons were also changed out during the life of the fort requiring more training and creating problems with accountability. District headquarters told Tilford, in a messaged dated 23 September 1867, to ship all his Sharps carbines and excess ammunition to Fort Union immediately, as they were being replaced by the Spencer carbine.

In January 1871 Lieutenant Colonel Thomas Devin, 8th Cavalry, reported, ". . . on hand after inventory no socks, only large trousers and overcoats."[53] Six months later he was still complaining. "There is not now on hand a single pair of socks, cavalry coveralls, or trousers and not a pound of soap or salt"[54] Some of the shortages were unexplained. On 4 January 1872 Captain Edmund G. Fechet, 8th Cavalry, opened two boxes supposedly holding thirty pairs of boots each, but the boxes were empty. He had signed for the boxes without actually counting the boots from Lieutenant Lawrence L. O'Connor who had since mustered out.

Fechet was asking for relief of pecuniary responsibility. He had learned the hard way to count everything before signing for it, something each officer and non-commissioned officer in the service has learned at one time or another.[55]

Shortages of food, clothing, and equipment were a problem for commanders and men throughout the history of Fort Selden, but despite that they always managed to accomplish their mission and keep the post operating.

## Feed for the Animals

Another priority under logistics was care and feeding the animals at the fort. The draft animals and cavalry mounts required extensive amounts of fodder and forage to maintain their stamina in moving supplies and chasing hostiles. The fifteen-square-mile post did not have sufficient grazing land to support the large number of animals, and the post was forced to buy corn, hay, and other fodder.

The number of animals at Fort Selden varied every month and every year depending on whether cavalry or infantry units occupied the post. Lieutenant Colonel Edward B. Willis, 1st New Mexico Infantry, reported in 1866 that when finished the corrals and stables would accommodate some 200 animals.[56]

The corrals must have been overflowing during those times that two cavalry troops were assigned to the post. For example, in May of 1872 Major Clendenin, 8th Cavalry, reported that he had 234 animals on hand:

> On hand 136 troop horses, 6 officer's horses, and 92 mules. Estimate we are using about 76,000 pounds of forage a month. We have enough on hand until July. Request a local contract for four months of corn.[57]

The fodder was provided through several local contractors. The *New Mexican* reported H.C. Herring of Las Cruces was the low bidder to provide fodder for the post in July 1868 at $14.95 per ton of gramma grass.[58] This is slightly less than the average price for hay of $16.50 a ton paid by other southwestern forts.[59] Other contractors provided hay and fodder for the post over the years, including Henry Lesinsky of Las Cruces, and John Lemon and Pedro Serna of La Mesilla.[60] Each of these contractors also contributed to the financial gain of the area by hiring laborers or subcontractors within the Mesilla Valley.

The amount of fodder used by the post was substantial. In June 1871, the inventory of hay and corn at Fort Selden was reported as 200,000 pounds of corn and 200 tons of hay. In December 1873, Major Clendenin, 8th Cavalry, had local contracts for 500,000 pounds of corn and 75,000 pounds of barley, but he had a problem with those amounts because his two cavalry units were being transferred to Fort Bayard.[61] With only infantry units at the post in 1874, the number of animals had dropped to four horses and forty mules with a comparable drop in fodder consumption. Major John S. Mason, 15th Infantry, reported to Santa Fe that the post now had 364,531 pounds of excess grain on hand.[62] The district quartermaster officer must have lost his sense of humor attempting to keep a balance between animals and fodder at the various forts.

H. C. Herring was again awarded the contract to provide 350 tons of hay at $12.63 per ton to Fort Selden upon the return of the units of the 9th Cavalry in 1875.[63] Herring continued to provide hay to Fort Selden at around $15 per ton for the next several years. When Lieutenant John Conline, 15th Infantry, held the post sale of excess property on the temporary abandonment in 1879, Herring bought back ninety-seven tons of hay for only $25.[64]

After reopening, the post was essentially an infantry post with little need for hay except to feed a small number of mules and transient animals. Captain Bascom, 13th Infantry, in December 1881, reported only thirty-one mules and one horse at the post.[65] The demand for local hay and fodder had dropped considerably, and to further reduce the local market, the post after 1881 was supplied with baled hay via rail from the Midwest.

The post had a small problem with fraud concerning hay in October 1870. Major Clendenin reported that the civilians delivering the hay to the post had been putting stones in the hay wagons to increase their weight."John Lemon and Peter Lerna [Pedro Serna] express great mortification and chagrin on this act of their employees" was the wording of the message sent to Santa Fe.[66] By November the hay had been reweighed and restacked, and 3,113 pounds of rocks had been removed. As a penalty the contractors were forced to provide 16,000 additional pounds of hay.[67]

Fort Selden, in order to cut expenses, attempted to produce baled hay in 1882. The post at this time was composed totally of infantry soldiers. The comments by the men, while baling hay in the heat and dust for the already detested cavalry units at other posts, must have been rather salty. The post was provided a Dederick Perpetual Baling Press and was expected to harvest the grass fields previously used to graze the beef herds. The results were not too successful. Captain Bascom reported that the machine was like a, "horrible pile driver and smashed the hay to dust."[68] He also encountered supply problems. "We have baled no hay. [as we] have not received wire."[69] When a supply of wire was received, the post had some minor success in the baling process. Bascom told headquarters in July 1882, that he had 631 bales ready for shipment, but the effort to grow fodder on the post seemed to fade after that.

**Transportation**

The animals that ate the fodder were the primary means of transportation for the post until the arrival of the railroad. Buckboards, spring wagons, freight wagons, and ambulances were the primary vehicles. The ambulance was used to transport officers and their families as it had a roof, sides, and seats.

Not only was transportation slow and undependable due to terrain and weather, but it was also hampered by the shortages of animals and wagons at Fort Selden. When Major Wilbur F. DuBois, 3rd

Cavalry, and his unit were ordered to Arizona, he listed the following troop property that had to be transported: 1,000 pounds of horseshoes; 1,150 pounds of nails; 21,600 rounds of ammunition; forty-six saddles, ninety sabers, the troop mess kit and all its "valuable crockery," and an 800 pound library.[70] He did not have sufficient wagons to carry the load and requested additional wagons from Santa Fe, but even with the additional wagons, some of the equipment had to be left behind.

Messages to and from the district headquarters indicated that transportation was always scarce at the post. In December 1871, Lieutenant Colonel Devin, 8th Cavalry, requisitioned "one (1) spring wagon" because the post was desperate for transportation.[71] In October 1872, Major Clendenin, 8th Cavalry, could not comply with an order from the District to send a certain number of wagons to Santa Fe. He outlined his problems:

> I have sent 5 wagons to Santa Fe for potatoes and butter. . . . [There are] insufficient mules for the sixth wagon. 12 mules shipped to Fort Cummings, 4 reserved for the inspector general. I have no more transportation.[72]

If the cavalry units had transportation problems, the infantry units must have had it even worse without assigned animals. They had to borrow or in some cases steal animals to help with their transportation needs. In December 1873 Major Clendenin, 8th Cavalry, reported that he had "no transportation available to help transfer Companies F and H, 15th Infantry, to Fort Selden."[73] The two companies must have received transportation assistance from elsewhere for they appeared on the Fort Selden monthly returns for January 1874. In November 1875, Captain Chambers McKibben, 15th Infantry, stated in response to a request: "The two six mule teams are at Blazers Mill [the sawmill in Tularosa] picking up lumber to repair the ferry . . . will not be able to transport troops."[74]

Transportation was also scarce during the temporary abandonment in 1878. Lieutenant William Cory, 15th Infantry, who was given the responsibility of shutting down the post, did not have sufficient transport to move the post's property to Fort Bliss and requested, "two more wagons to move excess stores to Fort Bliss."[75]

After the arrival of the railroad, the Fort Selden commanders still reported an inadequate number of wagons and teams. Captain Joseph G. Haskell, 23rd Infantry, wrote to Santa Fe in March 1883' ". . . need mules badly. The post only has one team for spring wagon capable of traveling more than 100 miles."[76]

Other groups also made demands on the post's slim transportation assets. In 1882, Professor George Davidson and the United States Coast and Geodetic Survey team used up all the post's wagons and mules when he set up a transit of Venus on Lookout peak in the Robledo Mountains. Lieutenant Jesse C. Chance, 13th Infantry, wrote the commander of Fort Stanton, "cannot provide you with transportation. All available is being used to transport the equipment for transit of Venus." [77]

Because of the constant shortage of transportation, the commanders of Fort Selden tended to "borrow" the wagons of other posts when they came to the post on other missions. In November 1872, Major Clendenin, 8th Cavalry, explained to the commander at Fort Cummings, "I used your ambulance to ship assistant surgeon Goodman to Fort Stanton. We have neither ambulance nor spring wagon." Obviously, neither did Fort Cummings after Clendenin commandeered it. In February 1877, Captain Carroll, 9th Cavalry, wrote the commander at Fort Bayard "your six mule team and wagon was sent to Fort Stanton. We will not replace it."[78]

Animal breakdown and sickness also contributed to the shortages of transportation. District headquarters in 1868 gave an indication of the problem with their instruction on packing mules:

> There is a great difference in using pack mules with troops without disabling them. Please pay attention to loads . . . only items authorized are outlined in special orders 117. Do not use the pack saddle known as "X." A [New] Mexican guide who understands packing must be taken on scouts.[79]

In 1873, an epidemic of horse and mule disease swept the United States and Fort Selden. Major Clendenin, 8th Cavalry, and his units at Fort Selden were affected. He first thought the disease, epizootic, would be quite mild compared to the results in the East, but he changed his mind when the disease disabled his stock:

> It is worse than I first anticipated. One of the water tank mule team has died, the others are so badly off they are unsafe to use . . . cannot select enough mules from the remaining herd to supply the garrison with water.[80]

The effects of the disease wore off in a month, but that month must have been a long one for those soldiers detailed to carry water up from the river to the post.

Another tragedy struck the post and its transportation facilities in June 1889 when a fire broke out in the corral. The roof and shades were constructed of brush, and the flames spread rapidly. The corral, seven mules, five horses, a spring wagon, an ambulance, a freight wagon, and two escort wagons were destroyed. Lieutenant Brett, 24th Infantry, stated that he now knew what Dante meant by his description of hell.[81] The post had received Johnson's Patent Force pumps to reduce fire danger in 1875, but since there was no mention of their use during the fire, the assumption is they were removed as excess property in 1878 when the fort was temporarily abandoned and never replaced.

Another transportation asset that was extremely important during floods and high water was the ferry across the Rio Grande. The ferry was built and installed by the army, then turned over to a civilian to operate on contract. According to a report in the Las Cruces *Thirty Four* in June 1880 the ferry, some fifty feet long and fourteen and one-half feet wide, was connected to each side of the river by a cable and was pulled by one to three men. The first contractor was John Martin, who also established the well at Aleman's station, and the last contractor was Adolphe Lea.

The ferry, as important as it was to traffic, spent a considerable amount of time under water or being rebuilt. Major Lane, 3rd Cavalry, borrowed tar from Fort Craig in 1869 to rebuild the ferry. The Santa Fe *New Mexican* in February 1871 reported that the ferry was sunk and filled with sand.[82] In June 1872 Major Clendenin, 8th Cavalry, annulled the ferry contract:

> Because of indolence, carelessness, he [the contractor] sunk the ferry. So the patrol could not get across for two days. . . .I gave the contract to two soldiers recently discharged from Fort Selden of good character.[83]

But the ferry sunk again in September. Captain Fechet, 8th Cavalry, informed the press that the high waters that drove him in from a scout also sunk the ferryboat and carried off the cable.[84] In early 1874 the ferry was damaged and had to be rebuilt, but there were no more reports of ferry problems until 1877. In 1877 Lieutenant William A. Cory, 15th Infantry, stated, ". . . after a long delay of low water and broken cable the ferry is again opened to public traffic."[85]

When it was afloat, the ferry provided a necessary service. An article in the Las Cruces *Borderer*, July 1874, reported, "The ferry must be kept busy these days . . . as all trains going west are compelled to cross at that point. Harring [L C. Herring of Las Cruces] is now running it."[86] An advertisement in the *Mesilla Valley Independent,* 30 June 1877, placed by Royal Yeaman, the operator, claimed that the ferry at Fort Selden would give "speedy passage across the river to passengers, animals, and trains." The final reported rebuilding was in 1879. The local press again commented on the progress of re-stretching the cable and rebuilding the ferry, this time by Adolphe Lea.

The ferry had gone out of business in late 1882. Captain Bascom, 13th Infantry, reported, "The post has no ferry or flat boat."[87] The military ferry had been an important facility for crossing the Rio Grande until a bridge was built across the river between La Mesilla and Las Cruces in the 1880s.

In addition to the ferry service road transport was also important to the region. General Carleton required the men of Fort Selden to establish roads to both Fort Cummings and to Fort Bayard, plus the post was built on the main north-south road of New Mexico, El Camino Real, the old Spanish trade route from Chihuahua, through El Paso del Norte to Santa Fe.

Colonel Orlando M. Poe, aide-de-camp to General William T. Sherman, Commanding the Army, visited Fort Selden while on an area assessment mission for the army in March 1881. His report on the road from Fort Cummings to Fort Selden was clear and concise.

> The road [coming west from the river] is composed of heavy sand until we reached the mesa of the Jornada, from which point the road was good until within 5 miles of Selden. . . . The last five miles down the mesa to the post was very sandy.[88]

It was also most assuredly, as it is even today, dusty, full of chuckholes, lined with ruts, and washed out at arroyos during the rainy season.

Commercial transportation included both stagecoach and freighters. Fort Selden was a stage stop, and the Southern Overland Express had both an office and stable located within the reservation. During the temporary abandonment, the stage company and the post trader were the only inhabitants. The post had two stages a week bringing mail, supplies, and passengers from 1865 to 1881, but Captain MacArthur, 13th Infantry, reported in June 1886 that the railroad provided the only transportation to the post.[89]

Prior to 1881 Fort Selden received most of its goods through military and civilian wagon trains and local freight haulers. The Las Cruces *Borderer* reported in 1871, ". . . an eighteen wagon train being formed up at Lesinky's . . . goods for Selden and Bayard." The railroad arrived in 1881 eliminating the long haul by mule and oxen teams. The short haul system still was needed because Fort Selden became a supply distribution point for the forts in southern New Mexico. In 1884 Ellis reported to the Department of Missouri, "[Fort Selden] acts as a supply point for Forts Bliss, Cummings, Florida Station [Deming], Craig, and San Marcial . . . and to Fort Stanton by wagon train."[90]

By 1886 the post had its own railroad siding and its own covered passenger-loading platform. Captain MacArthur, 13th Infantry, always doing what was best for the post and his troops, arranged with the AT&SF for his officers and men to travel at half fare to El Paso.[91] Thus El Paso, in addition to Las Cruces, became a town for the monthly drinking or shopping sprees and the weekend get-a-ways.

The post, seemingly always hampered by transportation short-falls, equipment shortages, and bad rations, nevertheless continued to function, and in spite of the problems accomplished its mission. The cost of shipping supplies from the eastern supply points caused Fort Selden to purchase much of its goods and services locally. Thus the fort from 1865–1881 became the area's largest customer, and cash flowed into the region. Though the post's local needs changed with the arrival of the railroad in 1881, some items such as wood, coal, and beef were still purchased from local vendors until the post closed in 1891. We can safely say that Fort Selden through it logistical needs had an important economic impact on the growth of the Mesilla Valley.

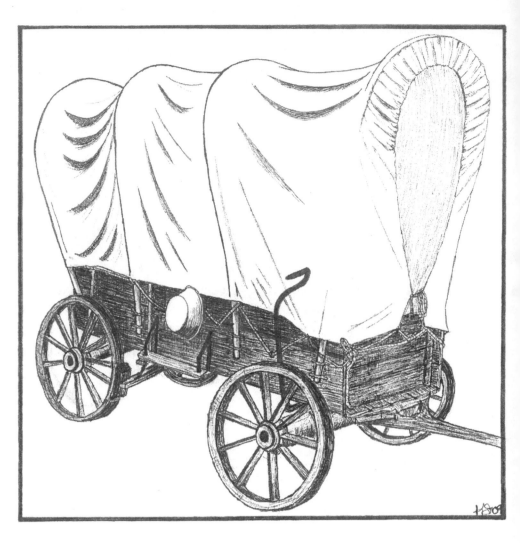

*Patrol Support Wagon*

*Ruins of Fort Selden*

# 5

# Relationships with the Local Communities

Previous chapters have indicated the military and economic importance of Fort Selden to the local communities. That importance was reflected in Fort Selden's role as a protector, employer, and creator of a local market, but the post and the surrounding communities had other forms of social interaction. The post in its early years functioned on several occasions as a social service office by providing food, medical support, and other benefits to the populace. It also served as a law enforcement agency providing support to the judges and the sheriffs of the communities and counties. The interactions and relations were not always peaceful as boundary disputes rose between the post and businessmen of the area, and conflicts for various reasons took place between the post commanders and the post traders. However, toward the end of the Indian wars the post changed roles from protector to sister community to share with others in more social interactions such as picnics, balls, and baseball games.

### Relief Efforts

The fort provided different forms of relief to the valley, but the most impressive was the direct issuance of food and seed in 1865 and 1866. The flood in the spring of 1865, followed by terrible hailstorms and "myriads of grasshoppers," had destroyed the crops of the local farmers.[1] General Carleton asked Lieutenant Colonel Davis, District Inspector General, and the officers at Fort Selden to become the relief center providing corn, seed, and flour for the "destitutes of the area."[2] The need for food throughout the Mesilla Valley was so great during these two years that Carleton wrote the Adjutant General of the Army asking for one million pounds of corn and one million pounds of flour to insure enough on hand to get the people through the year to the next crop. Carleton even bought mesquite beans to feed the animals at Fort Selden and the other posts under his command in order to conserve the grain for use by the people, but he found the horses preferred corn.[3]

Other relief efforts over the years included providing rations to destitute travelers, money and rations to those injured by army negligence, and medical aid. As early as 1863 the soldiers stationed at Las Cruces collected $245 to feed and clothe "orphan children."[4] In April 1866 Brevet Major William Brady, 1st New Mexico Volunteers, "issued four day's ration to a destitute civilian."[5] In 1874 the commander issued rations to the "Mexican" workers repairing the ferry cable "as they had nothing to eat."[6] As late as 1882 the post provided rations to four "destitute chinamen" en route to Fort Stanton.[7]

Fort Selden had numerous accidents involving weapons that resulted in payment or some form of recompense to the injured. Most of the accidents occurred among soldiers as discussed in Chapter 2 for whom no recompense was issued. For Example, on 29 December 1867, Corporal Nix was accidentally shot by one of his barracks mates, but luckily he recovered, and no recompense was authorized as he was taken care of by the post surgeon .[8] It was different for the civilians who were accidently injured or killed by stray bullets, or in some cases aimed bullets. Josefa Perez was accidentally shot during a change of guard in Mesilla in 1862 and had to have her leg amputated. General Carleton directed the Las Cruces quartermaster to provide her a day's ration "until further notice."[9] This order was then passed to Fort Selden in 1865, and according to Captain Tilford's message dated 11 February 1868, she was still receiving the ration in 1868. In another shooting incident, a post herder, Augustin Holguin, was mistaken for an Indian and was shot and killed during one of the numerous raids on the post herd. His daughter was awarded one ration a day, but the records do not reveal for what period.[10] Neither of these awards seems adequate compared to their loss and in view of today's standards, but with no relief programs in force they were quite generous for the times.

Medical support to the people of the Mesilla Valley was also important. The post surgeon and hospital facility provided assistance to both residents and travelers. Michael Foley from Dona Ana was treated for fevers in 1873, and Joseph Rich, a traveler, was treated and hospitalized after being found badly beaten on the post road in 1876.[11] In Rich's case, Captain Henry Carroll, 9th Cavalry, wrote to the Sheriff of Doña Ana County illustrating a problem for commanders. He felt morally bound to provide the medical support to civilians yet had to stay within the ever-present army regulations:

> Joseph Rich assaulted on 31 October by Manual Sisneros. The surgeon says Rich can now be moved. . . . I request that you take charge of him . . . army regulations prevent citizens from being retained in the hospital unless they cannot be moved.[12]

Felipe Lucero, who became the sheriff of Doña Ana County in the 1930s, remembered as a boy being thrown from his horse and severely injured while on a ride near the reservation. He was dazed and wandered around in the desert until discovered by "the men of the post who took him to the hospital."[13] In another incident, the post surgeon was called in April 1888 to help Juan Baca, a railroad worker, who had fallen under the wheels of a boxcar. He was placed in the Fort Selden hospital and the post surgeon was forced to amputate both legs. By the end of May the post surgeon reported that Juan Baca was "rapidly becoming convalescent."[14]

The surgeon sometimes did more for the citizenry than was deemed acceptable to the commander. In 1886 Captain Gregory Barrett, 10th Infantry, chastised the surgeon about having his own practice at the fort treating the area's civilians, "You will make instant records of the amount and types of Army Medications that you have issued to civilians."[15]

Another form of support the post provided was to the sheriffs and other law officials of the region, including arrests, escorting civilian prisoners to Santa Fe, and employing troops in population control measures. Officers at the post also provided information that assisted lawmen in making arrests. In 1868 Captain Tilford, 3rd Cavalry, reported to William Jones, deputy U.S. Marshal in Las Cruces, "Washington Hyde for whom you hold a warrant is now in Leasburg."[16] In reciprocal actions the lawmen helped recover stolen military goods and deserters. The lawmen were, in many cases, monetarily rewarded for their assistance. In May 1870, J.L. Hull, "Deputy U.S. Collector" in El Paso, arrested some thieves and recovered three mules stolen from Fort Selden. For this act, the post commander, Major David R. Clendenin, 8th Cavalry, recommended that he receive $175. On this evidence it seems that mules were more valuable than men because thirty dollars was the most paid to return a deserter.

There was also evidence of lack of cooperation at times between the post and the local law enforcement officers and messages from the post became somewhat heated over that fact. In March 1870 Captain Edmund G. Fechet, 8th Cavalry, could not get the sheriff to act so he wrote Judge Bailey, 3rd judicial district: "Fort Selden had four mules stolen. . . . They were trailed to Doña Ana where the trail was obliterated. . . . The mules were found in Las Cruces. Is it not a crime to steal from the United States?"[17]

In one case a civilian request for support left the post commander a trifle uneasy. On 6 February 1867, Edwin Orr, a judge in Las Cruces, asked Captain Tilford, 3rd Cavalry, "What type of assistance could the post provide?" Tilford wrote in reply, "We are bound to assist [you] especially to chastise Indians and thieves, but you must remember how jealous citizens are of their rights and of any encroachment on them."[18] Another interesting request should have left the commander uneasy as it appears that United States property was made available to a civilian. Major Lane, 3rd Cavalry, lent a number of his unit's weapons with ammunition to W. L. Rynerson of Las Cruces for security to establish a community near old Fort Thorn (Hatch).[19] There was no evidence that Lane informed headquarters of this, so it may have been a loan between friends.

The recovery of kidnapped Native American children was another mission that could raise the hackles between the military and the populace. A family in La Mesilla was keeping a Navajo girl as a servant, and General Carleton directed Captain Tilford in January 1867 to recover the girl. Tilford worked very carefully through Judge John Lemon in La Mesilla, and with his help was finally able to return the girl to her people in Bosque Redondo in April 1867 without bloodshed.[20]

The indentured servant problem arose several times in reports to headquarters, but the most serious clash was with a very prominent Las Cruces citizen, Martin Amador. On 22 June 1865, the New Mexican reported Captain John Thayer had Martin Amador brought under military escort to the Provost Marshal's Office in Las Cruces where Amador was then confronted with his indentured servant. Thayer, in front of Amador, told the servant "she was free to go where she pleased."[21] In another incident Lieutenant Colonel Davis, Inspector General, and Captain Whitlock, the first commander of Selden, exchanged words because Whitlock had allowed, "Don Pedro Garcia to retain and take in his charge his peon, Antonio Rodriquez."[22] The officers of Fort Selden were attempting to enforce the recently passed thirteenth amendment.

The riot in La Mesilla in 1871 demonstrated a different scenario in civil-military relations as the soldiers were used as police. The Las Cruces Borderer reported that "prompt action by General [Lieutenant Colonel Thomas C.] Devin, Major [Captain William] Kelly, and Lieutenant [Edward A.] Godwin, [all members of the 8th Cavalry Regiment] prevented more deaths and handled [the situation] with delicate yet efficient manner," and served to restore peace.[23] The fight, fueled by the approaching local elections, occurred after simultaneous political rallies of both the Republican and the Democratic parties

The two factions ended their political rallies with parades through the plaza about three o'clock Sunday afternoon 27 August 1871. As the two groups came close to each other they shouted insults and exchanged dire threats. The Santa Fe *New Mexican* reported, "Kelly a late employee in the *Borderer*'s office made an unprovoked attack with a heavy club upon Judge John Lemon . . . killing him."[24] The *Borderer* saw the fight somewhat differently as it reported on September 6, 1871,

"Mr. Kelly noted here as a peaceful man, unarmed approached Mr. Lemon in a most peaceful manner. It is believed that he [Kelly] was shot before he struck [Lemon] his whole dying energized in the blow [to Lemon]."

No matter where the truth lay, La Mesilla had a full-fledged battle raging in its streets with six killed and dozens more injured. The dead included John Lemon, L. N. Kelly (who was shot instantly after or before striking Lemon depending on the version), Sotillo Lopez, Francisco Rodriquez, Felicito Lucero, and Fabian Cordes [Cortez]. With the battle raging in and around the square in La Mesilla, an express rider was sent to Fort Selden for help. Devin, who had been in La Mesilla earlier that day and was about halfway back to the post, was overtaken by the rider, warned, and went on to Fort Selden to alert the troops.[25] Devin, Colonel J. Irwin Gregg, Deputy Commander of the District who was holding a court-martial at Fort Selden, Major John W. Brewer, the post surgeon, and sixty troopers arrived in La Mesilla after a two-hour-and-fifty-minute gallop from Fort Selden. The soldiers placed themselves between the warring factions and the shooting stopped. Devin and his troops bivouacked in the plaza overnight to insure no more outbreaks between the two groups. He reported to Santa Fe that the fighting had continued from 3:00 PM to 9:00 PM on Sunday, but that "No disturbance took place on Monday so half of the troops were sent back to Fort Selden, and the others were moved to a more suitable location to overlook the funerals."[26] No further incidents occurred, and the remaining troopers returned to Fort Selden on 3 September 1871.

However, the La Mesilla population was still a bit nervous. On 4 September 1871, Devin replied to a request for troops from "Mssrs.

Reynolds and Griggs" in La Mesilla:

> Troops are not necessary for the preservation of life and property. The election is over. . . . Should civil authority need help on the day that the election results are announced. I will readily cooperate with them in the maintenance of peace and good order.[27]

But it seems that cooler heads prevailed, and no further assistance was necessary. The only problem for Devin was that he now had to answer to Santa Fe about, "The necessity for calling out the troops and by whose authority they were called out."[28] This message raises two interesting questions. First, was the communications lag that bad? Devin committed troops on 27 August 1871, reported it to Santa Fe on 30 August with another follow-up message on 8 September, yet did not get the reprimand message until 30 September. Second, why did headquarters chastise him if the deputy district commander was on hand during the deployment of troops? Perhaps a higher command had questioned the prudence of such an act, and Santa Fe just let the message roll downhill.

## Boundary Disputes

Soon after Lieutenant Colonel Davis surveyed the sixteen-square-mile reservation of Fort Selden in early 1865, the town of Leasburg sprang up. Adolphe Lea had laid claim to a quarter section (160 acres) to establish his businesses in the area. This claim actually overlapped a small portion of the southern boundary of the reservation. The commanders fought the intrusion of this town on their post, but never were able to solve the problem.

Lieutenant Colonel Alexander Duncan, 125th Infantry, wrote to district headquarters for help in November 1866.

> Leasburg is a curse to this post as the cemetery records show. . . . Seven or eight soldiers have been murdered there. . . . It is on the reservation. Drives soldiers crazy from the effects of poisonous

liquor. . . . Mr. Lea is a respectable and honest man, but his town is primarily liquor sellers, gamblers, and prostitutes.[29]

Captain Joseph G. Tilford, 3rd Cavalry, requested a new survey of the post in 1868. "No commander can insure discipline or preserve good order. The town of Leasburg is selling mean whiskey and purchasing government arms and equipment."[30] He demeaned Judge Hackney's description of Leasburg by saying, "He calls it a town . . . if two groggeries and twice that number of houses of prostitution constitute a town."[31]

In early 1868 the army sent a surveyor, Captain John Rziha, a staff engineer with the 37th Infantry, "to lay off the reservation at your post."[32] After checking records in the Land office, he found that Adolphe Lea's claim was valid, and resurveyed a line, which cut off that portion of the post. The resurveyed boundary was forwarded to Washington for approval, but in the interim Major Clendenin, 8th Cavalry, was still having troubles with Leasburg and asked the district commander for a swift decision:

> Mr. Adolphe Lea in company with his lawyer Hackney lay claim to a portion of the post. Leasburg is a nest of thieves, harlots, and whiskey vendors. . . . It causes three quarters of the sickness on post . . . induces soldiers to steal stock and other property from the post.[33]

The boundary was formally changed in November 1870 when President Ulysses S. Grant approved the new survey that left Fort Selden with fifteen square miles instead of the original sixteen. The boundary problems with Leasburg were settled, but the other problems of alcohol, prostitution, and gambling at Leasburg would not subside until Lea became the post trader in 1881. Then the problems only changed location.

The commanders of Fort Selden had other boundary disputes. The first was with the railroad. The railroad came through the reservation in 1881, and its right-of-way gave permission to quarry rock on all public land except Indian or military reservations.[34] In 1885 AT&SF crews began digging rock on the reservation to repair some washed out track. Captain MacArthur, 13th Infantry, discovered their work on 30 January. In a message to the railroad superintendent at San Marcial, he stated: "You are removing rock from Fort Selden reservation. . . . Until approval is received suggest you suspend your operations."[35] Approval from district headquarters allowed the railroad crews to take 25,000 cubic yards of stone from the northern portion of the reservation, but MacArthur had the final word: "Your men are subject to military authority while on the reservation."[36] The quarry on Fort Selden was reopened in August 1885, but MacArthur's only worry this time was that all of "the workers would be vaccinated prior to their entry on the reservation."[37]

To provide entertainment for the crews digging and hauling rock, Morgan and Company of Las Cruces decided to build a saloon close by, but the location selected encroached on the post. MacArthur wrote to "Mssrs Morgan and company" about their house of entertainment on Van Patten's ranch. "You must move one half mile south of the railroad station. . . . Otherwise you will be forcibly removed."[38] He also informed Eugene Van Patten, sheriff of Doña Ana County that he was encroaching, "The boundary markers [of the reservation] have disappeared, but your ranch is on the reservation."[39] Finally on 16 February 1885, MacArthur applied to the engineers at Fort Leavenworth for help. "I am having problems with encroachment request a survey team to reestablish Fort Selden boundaries."[40] While the discussion between MacArthur and Van Patten continued, the saloon flourished.[41] But when the washout had been repaired, rock was no longer needed, the saloon closed along with the quarry. The question of the boundary with Van Patten's ranch must have gone away peaceably also because the Fort Selden boundaries were not resurveyed in the 1880s.

The last encroachment occurred as the post had started to close. Lieutenant James Brett, 24th Infantry, had received a "be prepared to" remove any remaining army material and equipment and turn the buildings and grounds over to the Department of Interior.[42] Others must have also received the word the post was closing because on 25 March

1889, Brett reported that a group of citizens had begun to dig a ditch across the southern part of the reservation. The Mesilla Valley Land and Irrigation Company was attempting to bring water from the Rio Grande to the northern portion of the Mesilla valley. Brett sent a message to the company stating that "No digging would be permitted until the post was formally turned over to the Department of the Interior."[43] But local pressure to allow digging continued, and in June Brett told H. H. Llewellyn of Las Cruces: "I have sent your request to dig an irrigation ditch across the post to the proper authorities."[44]

Then a mix up in communications occurred. The irrigation company had approval from the Department of Arizona, but Brett had received no word. In December Brett wrote Llewellyn again, "I understand approval was received on 19 December. . . . All work must stop until I see the telegram and your license."[45] The documentation must have been in order for Brett soon reported to the Department that "work has commenced. . . . The ditch will undoubtedly bring many settlers to the Mesilla Valley and enhance the value of property."[46]

In its 28 December issue, the Las Cruces *Rio Grande Republican* reported that work was going fast on the big canal with eighty teams scraping and digging. But in January 1890 the War Department overruled the decision by the Department of Arizona, and Brett was forced to tell Llewellyn one more time that "work on the ditch must stop."[47] The ditch was finally dug, but after the post had closed.

## Troubles with the Post Trader

The post trader, or sutler, provided a valuable service to the military post. The post store sold sundries, food, alcohol, and provided a place for the soldiers to play cards and billiards, and according to some of the commanders cavort with women. There were several post traders during Selden's history, John Blake, E.F. Kellner, Morehead, but the longest in tenure was Adolphe Lea from 1881 until closure in 1891.[48] The traders frequently ran afoul the post commander.

Several times the trader was accused of purchasing military

equipment and stores. On 3 January 1868, Private Isham Logan, Company K, 38th Infantry, was found guilty of trading his military clothing in return for a dozen eggs.[49] Supposedly, Logan had sold his clothing to the post trader, but that allegation could not be proven. On 5 July 1868, Captain Tilford, 3rd Cavalry, wrote to the trader, ". . . . The ten shocks of corn delivered to your clerk were stolen from our corral."[50] In another incident a private reported seeing Tilford hand John Martin a brand new army Spencer carbine, and later the carbine was seen in the possession of Hugh Axtel, a civilian working for the stage company. The soldier was court-martialed for making disparaging remarks against the commander and trader.[51] There was no indication that the district had overturned the conviction of the private, but they must have believed the accusation for Captain Tilford was transferred.

The trader was also accused several times of violating post regulations of the sale of alcohol. At times the commanders went so far as to limit the number of drinks that a man could buy. Major Lane ordered the trader, "You will sell to the ordnance sergeant no more than two drinks a day."[52] The post adjutant, Lieutenant Smith, gave instructions to E.F. Kellner, the post trader in October 1875, to "sell liquor by the drink only to soldiers and camp followers."[53] In 1876 the post adjutant under Captain Carroll's orders closed the store. "You are selling liquor to the enlisted men of this command while they are intoxicated. . . . You are instructed to close."[54] One commander had instituted "blue laws" during his tenure, "Close your store on Sunday."[55] Captain MacArthur had to reprimand the trader in June 1883, "Mr. Lea [who was now the post trader], drinks are allowed by glass only. Stop the sale of liquor by the bottle to enlisted men and employees." MacArthur also reminded Lea that store hours were from 6:30 AM until 8:45 PM and cited the department circular that governed the stores operations. Lea must have adhered to the regulation and stopped the practice at least until the arrival of a new commander. Captain Barrett, 10th Infantry, had to remind Lea in 1887:

Selling beer, whiskey, or wine by the bottle is strictly prohibited.

None of these spirits will be sold to a drunk soldier. Sell by glass only—an ordinary drink in a glass to be drunk at your counter.[56]

Then again in 1888, Barrett wrote to Lea: "You have disobeyed my order. Why do you sell whiskey of the vilest character?"[57]

The trader was also accused several times of "keeping" women in his establishment. Captain Tilford had to respond to the district commander on a complaint from "Judge" A.H. Hackney of Leasburg that John Blake, the post trader, was keeping prostitutes at the "sutler's store."[58] The district commander must have sided with Hackney and Lea. because this incident along with the weapon donation to Mr. Martin ended with Tilford's re-assignment to Fort Reynolds in Kansas.

There were other problems between the post commander and the post trader. When Captain Carroll, 9th Cavalry, shut down the store over the alcohol problem, he also fired Kellner and hired Louis Bailey. Not only did this stop his mail (Chapter 3, Communications), it also created a "who's in charge problem." Only the Adjutant General of the Army had the authority to remove the post trader, and Kellner appealed by letter to the Secretary of War over his firing.[59] This feud with the trader continued until December, when Kellner offered to resign in favor of Morehead.[60] Fort Selden had two post traders and lots of confusion for a while.

The post trader also received criticism from the surgeon. The surgeon in January 1875 reported that the walk in front of the trader's store presented a, "disreputable appearance from slop" thrown from the store's dining room.[61] Kellner was still refusing to police the front of his store in September, but this time it was the commander complaining about the amount of refuse.[62]

Even though relations between the commanders and the various post traders seemed to be strained at times, the store was a necessity for the post and its soldiers.

**Parties and Baseball Games**

With the decline of the Apache threat and lawlessness, the

relationship between the post and the surrounding communities became more relaxed and informal. It was as if the post were now just another settlement in the area. The local newspapers had a Fort Selden column, and baseball games, balls, and other celebrations between the post and communities were the vogue.

Katherine Stoes, a local historian writing in the 1950s, reported that the baseball games between the post and the teams of the valley were big social fetes. In July 1885, "a special car attached to the northbound train carried an excursion party of 100 fans, and bets were already being placed as the car was uncoupled at the Fort."[63] The final score of that game was 27 to 24 in favor of the fort.

Dances in the local communities referred to by the soldiers as "balles" or "fandangos" were well attended by the soldiers and officers of Fort Selden. Lieutenant Storey in a letter to his fiancée 18 October 1866 mentioned two dances.

> I have made two visits to Las Cruces and La Mesilla since I last wrote. I attended the church at Cruces on Sunday last. Was introduced to the Padre who by the way is quite a character, Sunday evening I went to the Fandango and played Monte with him. . . . I have an invitation to a Balle next week, in Las Cruces. Our Balles are great institutions. The last one I attended I danced with my spurs on sadly and unfortunately damaged the dress of a senorita.[64]

The Christmas or New Year's ball at Fort Selden became the event of the year, and these galas continued until the post was too short of personnel to support them. The Santa Fe *New Mexican* reported in its 7 January 1868 edition that the Christmas ball and supper was surprisingly fine, and the Virginia reel was danced with fervor. The gala New Year's dinner and dance in 1883 also received rave reviews in the Las Cruces *Rio Grande Republican*.

The ball was held in a beautifully decorated room, 120 by 20 feet.

> . . . a sumptuous meal was provided accompanied by free cigars
> and liquor. . . . The visitors danced until five o'clock AM when they
> had to catch the train south.[65]

The ball was held in the troop barracks with all the cots and kits moved
out.

The Fourth of July was also a day for fun and games and an
occasion to hear the resounding thunder of the post's 12-pound
cannon in a salute to the nation's birth. The local press reported that
the celebration in 1871 included the federal salute, the band playing
the national anthem, various races of both men and horses, greased
pig chase, followed that evening with a grand ball and a performance by
the chorus. The band in this case must have been the regimental band
borrowed from Santa Fe as Fort Selden never had its own band. In 1874
the post's officers were invited to Las Cruces for the big celebration of
the Fourth. The Las Cruces *Borderer* edition of 11 July 1874, reported
that:

> Lt's Conrad, Godwin, and the clerk from Fort Selden spent the
> 4th in Las Cruces. The welcome visit of these favorite soldiers
> mingling in the social festivities of the day with our citizens helped
> much to give pleasure to the occasion.

Thus in addition to the patrols, pickets, and purchases made
by the post to support the communities of the Mesilla Valley, Fort
Selden was an important source of social services for the people. Fort
Selden's various commanders and troop units supported the local law
enforcement agencies, provided medical services, and even rations in
emergencies. As its role as protector slowly faded over the years, Fort
Selden was accepted as a sister community in the Mesilla Valley. Fort
Selden became just another town with whom to share baseball games,
holiday galas, and fun.

*Ruins of Fort Selden*

# 6

# Death of a Fort

Fort Selden had fought the Apaches, rustlers, post traders, and trespassers, but it lost its major battle to Fort Bliss, a sister post in El Paso some 70 miles to the south. With the arrival of the railroad in 1881 the army prepared to close the small inefficient, uneconomical two company posts that were spread throughout the Southwest. The railroad provided a system of rapid transport of troops to places of need, which allowed the army to consolidate units into regimental posts of twelve companies.

Fort Selden was initially selected as one of these regimental posts. General Phillip H. Sheridan, commanding the Division of the West, stated:

> I have examined the site of Fort Selden and it is a superb one for a post of any size. Troops can easily be sent by rail to Fort Wingate and by connecting rail to many other points. . . . Respectfully recommend that the post to be built in New Mexico be located at this point.[1]

General William T. Sherman, commanding the army, sent his aide-de-camp, Colonel Orlando Poe, to reconnoiter the area and present his selection of the best site. Poe's message to Sherman in March 1881 revealed his indecision.

It [Fort Selden] has been a pretty post . . . the adobe buildings would now be in good condition had they not been dismantled to get the woodwork for use at Fort Bliss. . . . If the reservation at Bliss was as good as this I would consider the whole question settled.[2]

In his recommendation to Sherman he listed Fort Selden first in availability, but Fort Bliss first in "military implications" because of the four railroads into El Paso and its closeness to the border with Mexico.

Even with Poe's indecision the question seemed settled. Sheridan was adamant that the Fort Selden site was the best because it was available, and construction could start immediately. The army went ahead with plans for the construction of a regimental post at Fort Selden. The plans were drawn up and finalized in January 1882.[3] The new Fort Selden was to have buildings built of brick or stone. There were several new buildings proposed, including the regimental headquarters, six large barracks, two sets of quarters for field grade officers, 12 double (duplexes) quarters for company grade officers, a hospital, and large stable and corral area. In March 1882 President Chester A. Arthur forwarded to Congress a request for $251,451.69 to rebuild Fort Selden.[4] A local newspaper was ecstatic about the decision. The Las Cruces Borderer had advanced news on this item. In June 1881 the paper reported:

Fort Selden is to be made a twelve company post. . . .Fort Selden is handy to the railroad, is centrally located, and offers special advantages as a supply post. . . .If this change is made it will help Las Cruces to no small degree.[5]

But General Sherman was still not convinced that Fort Selden was the answer and made his own reconnaissance in 1882. After visiting every site from San Antonio to Santa Fe, he came to the same conclusion of Poe that even though the Fort Bliss reservation was much smaller than

Fort Selden, it had access to more railroads. To Sherman the mobility provided by the four connecting railroads was more important than "the fort, town, or anything else in this quarter."[6] By 11 May 1882, he had convinced the Secretary of War, Robert Lincoln, and a message was sent to Congress. "Please withdraw Fort Selden [from consideration]. General Sherman has recently made an inspection tour and feels that it would be better to build at El Paso."[8] Fort Selden had lost its first, only, and most important battle.

The post continued in service for nine more years but as a supply depot and as a sub post of Fort Bayard, New Mexico. Lieutenant James E. Brett, 24th Infantry, the last commander, sent the final message from the post on 20 January 1891. "All public property from this post having been disposed of it [Fort Selden] was abandoned this date."[9]

The abandonment of Fort Selden also meant leaving many fallen comrades behind. The post cemetery in 1885 had a total of 103 graves. Captain MacArthur, 13th Infantry, in an attempt to clean up the cemetery had requested help from the district in repairing the grave markers, ". . . need help . . . headboards need replacing."[10] He went on to list the graves, "33 soldiers, 1 Indian Scout, 59 unknowns, and 10 citizens." In 1888, Captain Barrett, 10th Infantry, again reminded Washington of the graves at Fort Selden. "Capt Henry Stanton [for whom Fort Stanton was named] killed in 1855 now interred at Fort Selden. Request transfer to the National Cemetery [Santa Fe]."[11]

When the fort was finally closed, the remains of Captain Henry Stanton, the other soldiers, and the scout were moved to Santa Fe. The known civilians were reinterred in local cemeteries, while the 59 unknown are still interred somewhere between the current State Monument and the river.[12] Dorothy Seager reported that," . . . in payment for his services the person who exhumed the bodies of the military dead and transported them to Santa Fe was given the right [to remove] the wood structure's pieces."[13] How much of the fort's wood structures were left is a mystery because Colonel Poe had reported that all frames, both window and doors had been removed to build quarters at Fort Bliss.

Fort Selden had entered the arena late in the war against the Apache in the Southwest, and because of its important location it lasted twenty-six years. This was a longer period of service than any of the other forts along the Rio Grande, such as Forts Thorn (Hatch, NM), Fillmore, Craig, McCrea, and Cummings. The Southwest had changed in those twenty-six years. The Southwest was more populated, the Indian wars were over, and the railroads now crossed the land providing rapid access to most parts of the land.

Fort Selden and the many soldiers that served there contributed in no small way to the overall security and economical development of the Mesilla Valley. Its commanders and soldiers had patrolled the region, recovered lost stock, and defended the citizens of the Mesilla Valley to the best of their ability. As Robert Utley stated, the "men in blue" had faced an extremely tough job and accomplished it "with a mix of wisdom and stupidity, selfless dedication and mindless indifference".[14] And so it was with the units at Selden, one day shooting down a defenseless herder and the next giving up a soldier's life to protect a citizen.

As important as the Fort Selden patrols were to pacification, the fort through its need for supplies and services had injected money into the local economy and created jobs and a market. Thus the fort became the largest cash investor in the Mesilla Valley until the arrival of the railroad, and after 1881 the fort was still important to the local economy. This was not unique as Francis Prucha, Robert Frazer, and Darlis Miller have shown. The army posts of the West have had a great influence on the growth of the western communities and regions. Fort Selden by contributing its manpower, money, and time to the Mesilla Valley presents a good example of the effects of the southwestern posts on the local communities.

Even in its final years, after the decision had been made to close the post, Fort Selden provided social relief from the humdrum of frontier living, with galas and baseball games. Its final gift to the Mesilla Valley was the excess equipment and supplies auctioned off to local people as they bid on the remaining lumber, vigas, and supplies that were too heavy or too expensive to ship to other posts. Fort Selden's military utility was gone. Today, its deteriorating walls stand as a monument to the many soldiers and units that served the citizens of the Mesilla Valley and the Southwest.

# Notes

## Chapter 1

1. James C. McKee, Narrative of the Surrender of a Command of U.S. Forces at Fort Fillmore, NM (Houston: Stage Coach Press, 1960), 29.

2. Santa Fe New Mexican, 13 October 1865.

3. Darlis A. Miller, "General James Henry Carleton in New Mexico, 1862–1867," Master's Thesis: New Mexico State University, 1970), 35.

4. Letters Sent, Department of New Mexico, Record Group 393, Microfilm Series 1072, Roll 3, National Archives (LS, DNM, RG 393, M-1072, Roll 3, NA), General Carleton to General Thomas, 22 February 1864.

5. Ibid., General Carleton to General Thomas, 30 September.

6. Ibid., General Carleton to Colonel West, 5 March 1863.

7. Ibid., General Carleton to Adjutant General, War Department, 1 February 1863.

8. Ibid.

9. Santa Fe New Mexican, 4 November 1964.

10. Ibid., 3 June 1864.

11. LS, DNM, RG 393, M-1072, Roll 3, NA, General Carleton to General West, 8 October 1862, and General Carleton to Cristobal Ascarate, 25 February 1864. He had also promised this to the civic leaders of the southern communities.

12. Francis B. Heitman, Historical Register and Dictionary of the Army, volume 1, (Urbana: University of Illinois Press, 1965), 359.

13. LS , DNM, RG 393, M-1072, Roll 3, NA, General Carleton to General West, 19 June 1864.

14. Timothy Cohrs and Thomas J. Caperton, Fort Selden, New Mexico, (Santa Fe: Museum of New Mexico, 1974), 2.

15. T. M. Pearce, New Mexico Place Names: A geographical Dictionary, (Albuquerque: University of New Mexico Press, 1965), 77. The phrase in Spanish is more accurately translated as the "journey of the dead man" but the literal and most widely accepted version is:"journey of death".

16. LS, DNM, RG 393, M-1072, Roll 3, NA, General Carleton to Lieutenant Colonel Davis, 1 September 1865. A viga is straight wood pole, usually pine, used horizontally from wall to wall to support the roof

17. Medical Histories of Posts, Fort Selden, Record Group 94, Records of the Adjutant General, Microfilm Series-617, National Archives. (MH, FS, RG 94, M-617, NA) Surgeon's Annual Report, 31 December 1870.

18. LS, DNM, RG 393, M-1072, Roll 3, NA, General Carleton to General Thomas, 14 August 1865.

19. Ibid., General Carleton to Lieutenant Colonel Davis, 1 September 1865. Carleton sent several messages to his officers about their men drinking, gambling, and a laxity in the command.

20. Ibid., General Carleton to Captain Whitlock, 27 April 1865.

21. Ibid., General Carleton to Captain Whitlock, 23 May 1865.

22. Ibid., General Carleton to Colonel McFerran, 23 May 1865.

23. Letters Sent, Fort Selden, 1866–1890, Record Group 92, Records of the Quartermaster General, National Archives Microfilm. (LS, FS, RG 92, NA) Lieutenant Colonel Willis to Assistant Adjutant General, District of New Mexico, 17 June 1866.

24. Lydia S. Lane, I Married a Soldier: Old Days in the Old Army, (Albuquerque: Horn & Wallace, 1964), 171.

25. MH, FS, RG 94, M-617, NA, Monthly Sanitation Report, 21 February 1876.

26. LS, FS, RG 92, NA, Captain MacArthur to Assistant Adjutant General, Department of Missouri, 12 October 1884.

27. Las Cruces Rio Grande Republican, 30 November 1889.

## Chapter 2

1. Robert M. Utley, Frontier Regulars: The United States Army and the Indian, 1866–1891 (Lincoln: University of Nebraska Press, 1973), 14.

2. Ibid., 14.

3. Post Returns, Fort Selden, Returns from U.S. Military Posts, Record Group 94, 1800–1916, Microfilm Series M-617, Roll 1145, National Archives Microfilm (PR, FS, RG 94, M-617, Roll 1145, NA). 31 May 1865 and 31 August 1866

4. Santa Fe Gazette, 27 Mar 1869. The 38th Infantry Regiment merged with the 41st Infantry to form the 24th Infantry Regiment.

5. Don Ricky, Jr., Forty Miles a day on Beans and Hay: The Enlisted Soldier Fighting the Indian Wars (Norman: University of Oklahoma Press, 1973), 88.

6. Letters Sent, Fort Selden, Record Group 92, Records of the Quartermaster General, National Archives Microfilm, (LS, FS, RG 92, NA). Captain DuBois to Assistant Adjutant General, District of New Mexico, 15 December 1870.

7. Ibid., Captain Chance to the Commanding Officer, Fort Bliss, Texas, 18 September 1886. The Rio Grande must have been full from the rainy season that occurs in July and August.

8. Ibid., Captain Chilson to Assistant Adjutant General, District of New Mexico, 14 June 1884.

9. Ibid., Captain MacArthur to U.S. Land Office, Las Cruces, 5 July 1886.

10. Utley. 16.

11. PR, FS, RG 94, M-617, Roll 1146, NA, January through December 1872.

12. Ibid., January through December 1882.

13. Santa Fe New Mexican, 9 December 1873.

14. Letters Sent, Headquarters, Department of New Mexico/District of New Mexico, 1849–1890, Record Group 393, Records of the Continental Commands, Microfilm Series M-1072, National Archives Microfilm, (LS, DNM, RG 393, M-1072, NA). Major DeForrest to all posts, 23 April 1867.

15. LS, FS, RG 92, NA, Lieutenant Fitch to Assistant Adjutant General, District of New Mexico, 9 March 1870.

16. Ibid., Major William Lane to Assistant Adjutant General, District of New Mexico, 19 April 1869.

17. Ibid., Captain Stanwood to Assistant Adjutant General, District of New Mexico, 28 October 1869.

18. Ibid., Lieutenant Elting to Assistant Adjutant General, District of New Mexico, 11 October 1869.

19. United States Department of the Interior, Ninth Census of the United States, 1870, Population Schedules for New Mexico, Dona Ana County, Record Group 92, Microfilm Series M-593, Roll 893, National Archives Microfilm.

20. LS, DNM, RG 393, Roll 3, NA, General Carleton to Captain Whitlock, 25 October 1865.

21. Post Records, Fort Selden, January 1867–December 1875, RG 393, Records of the Continental Commands, National Archives Microfilm (PR, FS, RG 393, RCM, NA). These documents provided through the courtesy of Fort Selden State Monument.

22. Ibid., Court-Martial Records, 28 December 1868.

23. Ibid., Court-Martial Records, 23 March 1869.

24. Ibid., Court-Martial Records, 11 November 1868.

25. Ibid., Court-Martial Records, 3 January 1868

26. According to the Uniform Code of Military Justice, desertion is the intention to remain away from the place of duty, while absence without leave is a temporary absence, usually less than thirty days. Desertion carries a much heavier penalty than does AWOL.

27. Ibid., Court-martial Records, 21 May 1869. Williams had been reduced from First Sergeant by a previous board, which explains why he had a wife and quarters as a private.

28. LS, DNM, RG 393, M-1072, Roll 4, NA, Major Deforrest to Captain Tilford, 18 June 1867.

29. LS, FS, RG 92, NA, Lieutenant Thomas Davis to Commanding Officer, Fort Stanton, 9 September 1877.

30. LS, FS, RG 92, NA, Lieutenant Colonel Willis to Assistant Adjutant General, Department of New Mexico, 14 July 1866.

31. Ibid., Major Lane to the Commanding Officer, Ft Craig, 19 April 1869.

32. Ibid., Major Clendenin to Commanding Officer Fort Craig, 6 March 1873.

33. Ibid., Captain Fechet to Assistant Adjutant General, District of New Mexico, 11 April 1872.

34. Ibid., Major Lane to Commander, Troop F, 3rd Cavalry, 20 May 1869.

35. Ibid., Commanding Officer, Fort Selden, to Chief of Police, Albuquerque, 14 May 1885.

36. Hugh M. Milton II, Fort Selden: Territory of New Mexico, 1865–1890 (Las Cruces: Hugh M. Milton II, 1971), 14.

37. J.H.Storey, Letter to his fiancée, (courtesy of staff at Fort Selden), 18 October 1866.

38. LS, FS, RG 92, NA Lieutenant Elting to Assistant Adjutant General, District of New Mexico , 20 October 1868.

39. Medical Histories of the U.S. Military Forts, Fort Selden 1780–1891, Record Group 94, Office of the Adjutant General, National Archives Microfilm, ( MH, FS, RG 94, NA). Monthly Sanitation Report, 30 June 1888

40. LS, FS, RG 92, NA, Lieutenant Brett to Post Adjutant, Fort Bayard, 18 September 1890.

41. Borderer, 23 November 1872. Major Clendenin reported that Cadetta had been killed.

42. LS, FS, RG 92, NA, Major Clendenin to AG, District of New Mexico, 1 December 1872.

43. Ibid., Captain Ellis to Assistant Adjutant General, District of New Mexico, 22 December 1883.

44. PR, RCM, FS, RG 393, NA, Court-martial Records, 6 May 1869.

45. Ibid., 1 October 1868.

46. Ibid., 29 April 1869.

47. Ibid., 9 July 1868.

48. LS, FS, RG 92, NA, Captain Tilford to Assistant Adjutant General, District of New Mexico, 3 March 1868.

49. Ibid., Commanding Officer, Fort Selden, to Lieutenant Colonel Devin, 3 January 1876.

50. LS, FS, RG 92, NA, Capt MacArthur to General Bradley, 9 June 1885.

51. Las Cruces, Borderer, 29 June 1871.

52. William H. Leckie, The Buffalo Soldiers: A Narrative of the Negro Cavalry in the West (Norman: University of Oklahoma Press, 1967), 72.

53. LS, FS, RG 92, NA, Captain Bascom to Assistant Adjutant General, District of New Mexico, 7 June, 28 July, and 25 September 1882.

54. Ricky, 58.

55. Ibid., 76.

56. LS, DNM, RG 393, M-1072, Roll 4, NA, Lieutenant Colonel Davis to Commanding Officer, Fort Selden, 25 October 1865.

57. MH, FS, RG 94, M-617, NA, Monthly Sanitation Report, 27 April 1876.

56. Ibid., 30 August 1876.

59. Ibid., 31 January 1877.

60. Ibid., 24 April 1876.

61. Ibid., Annual Post Report, 21 December 1874.

62. Ibid., Monthly Sanitation Report, 27 April 1876.

63. Las Cruces Thirty-Four, 18 May 1880.

64. Ibid., 11 February 1880.

65. PR, RCM, FS, RG 393, NA, Court-martial Records, 28 May 1867.

66. Ibid., 2 July 1869.

67. LS, FS, RG 92, NA, Captain Carroll to Assistant Adjutant General, District of New Mexico, 14 June 1876.

68. Ricky, 51.

69. LS, FS, RG 92, NA, Captain Tilford to Lieutenant Rigg, 22 January 1867.

70. Ibid., Captain MacArthur to Assistant Adjutant General, District of New Mexico, 30 March 1884.

71. Ibid., Lieutenant Colonel Devin to Assistant Adjutant General, District of New Mexico, 23 March 1871.

72. Merril J. Mattes, Indians, Infants, and Infantry: Andrew and Elizabeth Burt on the Frontier (Lincoln: University of Nebraska Press, 1988).

73. A copy of this invitation is found in Lieutenant Storey's papers. Courtesy of the Ft. Selden staff.

74. Lydia S. Lane, I Married a Soldier: Old Days in the Old Army (Albuquerque: Horn and Wallace, 1964), 172.

75. Ibid., 175.

76. LS, FS, RG 92, NA, Captain MacArthur to Adjutant General, Washington, DC, 14 February 1883.

77. MH, FS, RG 94, M-617, NA, Monthly Sanitation Report, 31 March and 30 June 1886.

78. Lane, 171.

79. Santa Fe New Mexican, 15 July 1873.

80. PR, RCM, FS, RG 393, NA, Court-Martial Records, 9 July 1868.

81. Ibid., 2 April 1869.

82. Santa Fe New Mexican, 2 March 1866, 2.

83. LS, FS, RG 92, NA, Lieutenant Robinson to Mr. Ketchum, 15 October 1869.

84. Ibid., Captain MacArthur to Assistant Adjutant General, Fort Leavenworth, 2 April 1884.

85. Ibid., to Adjutant General, Wash. DC, 6 May 1884.

86. Ibid., 10 September 1884.

87. Lane, 183. Webster's New World Dictionary defines a melodean as a small keyboard organ with pedals to operate the bellows.

88. LS, FS, RG 92, NA, Captain Barrett to Lieutenant Clarke, 28 June 1887.

89. Las Cruces Rio Grande Republican, 7 July 1883.

90. MH, FS, RG 94, NA. Monthly Sanitation Report, 30 April 1885. The building at this spring, now called Radium Springs, has been a bath house, women's prison, a restaurant, and is now abandoned.

## Chapter 3

1. Letters Sent, Ft. Selden, Record Group 92, National Archive Microfilm (LS, FS, RG 92, NA.) Captain Henry Carroll to Assistant Adjutant General, District of New Mexico, 20 July 1876.

2 Ibid., Captain Carroll to Commanding Officer, Fort Wingate, 28 November 1876.

3. Las Cruces Borderer, 18 May 1871, 2

4. Letters Sent, Department of New Mexico, Record Group 393, Series M-1072, Roll 3, National Archives Microfilm. (LS, DNM, RG 393, M-1072, Roll 3, NA). General Carleton to General West, 6 August 1863. Even though this message was sent before the building of Ft Selden, it is a good example of the type of instructions given to patrol leaders.

5. LS, FS, RG 92, NA, Captain Henry Carroll to patrol leader Davenport, 11 February 1877. Ojo Caliente (Hot Springs) was a temporary reservation for the Ojo Caliente Apaches north of Winston on Hwy 52. This was the home of Victorio, Geronimo, and Cochise in the early 1870s.

6. Ibid., Captain Brady to Assistant Adjutant General, Department of New Mexico,

5 April 1866. Captain Brady later became the sheriff of Lincoln County, New Mexico, and was shot and killed by William Bonny during the Lincoln County War.

7. Patrol Report from Lieutenant Henry Storey to Brevet Major DeForrest, Assistant Adjutant General, Department of New Mexico, 18 September 1866. (A copy of this letter is on file at Fort Selden). The Spring "Caresa" was probably Rope Springs at the base of San Andres Peak which is still a viable water source. When Storey referred to Mexicans we assume he meant Hispanics. Many reports and letters referred to San Andreas, the accepted spelling is San Andres.

8. Ibid.

9. LS, FS, RG 92, NA, Captain Chilson to Major Price, District of New Mexico, 17 July 1873.

10. Dan L. Thrapp, Victorio and the Mimbres Apache, (Norman: University of Oklahoma Press, 1974), 160. The difference in spelling of Cpl. Battling's name is probably the fault of this author with the difficulty in deciphering microfilm. Cañada Alamosa is a large canyon north of present day Truth or Consequences.

11. LS, FS, RG 92, NA, Captain Russell to Assistant Adjutant General, Department of New Mexico, 16 September 1868.

12. Ibid., Major Lane to Commanding Officer, Fort Bliss, 23 May 1869.

13. Ibid., Captain Carroll to Assistant Adjutant General, District of New Mexico, 18 September 1876.

14. LS, DNM, RG 393, M-1072, Roll 3, NA, General Carleton to Commanding Officer, Fort Selden, 20 June 1865.

15. Ibid., Major DeForrest to Captain Tilford, 24 September 1867. Mora is a small town northwest of Las Vegas, NM

16. Santa Fe New Mexican, 2 November 1867.

17. LS, DNM, RG 393, M-1072, Roll 3, NA, Assistant Adjutant General, Department of New Mexico to Commanding Officer, Fort. Selden, 11 May 1866.

18. Santa Fe New Mexican, 8 September 1866, 2.

19. Ibid., 3 December 1867, 2.

20. Post Returns, Fort Selden, 1865–1891, Record Group 94, Records of the Adjutant General, Microfilm Series M-617, Roll 1145, National Archives Microfilm. (PR, FS, RG 94, M-617, Roll 1145, NA), 19 November 1868.

21. Las Cruces Borderer, 3 January 1872, Locals, 2.

22. LS, FS, RG 92, NA, Major David R. Clendenin to Assistant Adjutant General, District of New Mexico, 16 October 1872.

23. Santa Fe New Mexican, 8 September 1865, letters to the editor.

24. Ibid., 16 March 1869.

25. Ibid., 28 October 1875, 3

26. Ibid., 7 July 1869.

27. Ibid., 12 December 1871.

28. Ibid., 7 September 1871.

29. Ibid., 6 December 1871.

30. Thrapp, 131.

31. Ibid., 195-200.

32. Ibid., 220.

33. PR, FS, RG 94, M-617, Roll 1146, NA, 31 December 1880.

34. LS DNM, RG 393, M-1072, Roll 4, NA, Adjutant General, Fort Bayard to Lieutenant Cory, 17 August 1881.

35. LS, FS, RG 92, NA, Lieutenant Colonel Bloodgood to Assistant Adjutant General, District of New Mexico, 26 July 1869.

36. Santa Fe Weekly Gazette, 8 May 1869.

37. Santa Fe New Mexican, 11 May 1869.

38. LS, FS, RG 92, NA, Major Lane to Assistant Adjutant General, District of New Mexico, 8 May 1869.

39. Santa Fe Weekly Gazette, 22 May 69.

40. Santa Fe New Mexican, 14 July 1869.

41. LS, FS, RG 92, NA, Captain Fechet to Assistant Adjutant General, District of New Mexico, 12 September 1872.

42. Santa Fe New Mexican, 6 October 1872, 1

43. LS, FS, RG 92, NA, Captain Haskell to First Sergeant, Troop B, Shedd's Ranch, 30 April 1883.

44. Letter from Lieutenant Storey to Annie, 20 August 1866.

45. LS, DNM, RG 393, M-1072, Roll 3, NA, Assistant Adjutant General, Department of New Mexico, to Commanding Officer, Fort. Selden, 12 December 1866.

46. Ibid., Adjutant, District of New Mexico, to Commanding Officer, Fort Selden, 28 May 1867, 25 May 1868, 25 October 1868, and 23 May 1871.

47. Ibid., Assistant Adjutant General, District of New Mexico, to Fort Selden, 28 April 1871.

48. LS, FS, RG 92, NA, Captain Carroll to Commanding Officer, Fort Stanton, 1 April 1877.

49. LS, DNM, RG 393, M-1072, Roll 3, NA, General Carleton to John S. Watts, New Mexico Territory, 22 October 1863.

50. Santa Fe New Mexican, 19 July 1871, 1.

51. LS, FS, RG 92, NA, Captain DuBois to Assistant Adjutant General, District of New Mexico, 15 February 1870, and LS, DNM, RG 393, M-1072, Roll 4, NA, Assistant Adjutant General, District of New Mexico to Commanding Officer, Fort Selden, 3 March 1870.

52. Ibid., Major Lane to Assistant Adjutant General, District of New Mexico, 11 April 1869.

53. Ibid., Captain Hulhammer to Assistant Adjutant General, District of New Mexico, 21 October 1876.

54. Ibid., Lieutenant Cory to Postmaster General, 10 May 1878.

55. Ibid., Captain Carroll to Assistant Adjutant General, District of New Mexico, 29 April 1876.

56. Ibid., Captain Bascom to Assistant Adjutant General, District of New Mexico, 17 November 1882.

57. Ibid., Captain MacArthur to Superintendent, Western Union, 9 September 1885.

58. Ibid., Captain MacArthur to Assistant Adjutant General, Fort Bowie, Arizona, 18 April 1886. Fort Selden was under the Department of Arizona during the chase of Geronimo.

59. Robert M. Utley, Frontier Regulars: The United States Army and the Indian 1866–1891, (Lincoln: University of Nebraska Press, 1973), 387.

60. Hugh M. Milton, II, Fort Selden, Territory of New Mexico, (Las Cruces: Hugh Milton, 1971), 16. Since the San Andres and the Sacramento Mountains lie between Fort Selden and Fort Stanton, "direct to" does not seem possible.

61. LS, FS, RG 92, NA, Lieutenant Brett to Commanding Officer, Columbus Barracks, Ohio, 25 February 1889.

62. Ibid., Captain MacArthur to Assistant Adjutant General, Division of the Pacific, 15 June 1886.

63. The Posse Comitatus act enacted in 1878 would have prevented the use of military forces in this type of confrontation.

64. Don Ricky, Jr.,Forty Miles a Day on Beans and Hay: the Enlisted Soldier Fighting the Indian Wars, (Norman: University of Oklahoma Press, 1973), 88.

65. LS, FS, RG 92, NA, Post Adjutant to Commanding Officer, Troop B, 4th Cavalry 27 August 1883.

66. Court-Martial Records, Fort Selden, Post Records, 1867–1890, Record Group 94, National Archives Microfilm. (MSR, FS, RG 94, NA), 26 January 1869.

67. Medical Histories of the U.S. Military Posts, 1790–1916, Fort Selden, Record Group 94, Microfilm Series-617, National Archives Microfilm. (MH, FS, RG 94, NA), 22 June 1875.

68. MH, FS, RG 94, M-617, NA, 21 December 1874

69. Ibid., 24 February 1875

70. Ibid., 25 January 1876.

71. Ibid., Post Surgeon to the Post Adjutant, Fort Selden, 25 January 1876

72. CMR, FS, PR RG 94, NA, 14 September 1869

73. LS, FS, RG 92, NA, Lieutenant Colonel Devin to Assistant Adjutant General, District of New Mexico, 1 September 1871.

74. Ibid., Major Clendenin to Assistant Adjutant General, District of New Mexico, 28 May 1872.

75. LS, FS, RG 92, NA, Commanding Officer, Fort Selden to Commander, Troop A 8th Cavalry, 8 June 1872.

76. Ibid., Captain Ellis to Assistant Adjutant General, District of New Mexico, 15 October 1882.

77. MH, FS, RG 94, M-617, NA, Post Surgeon to Commanding Officer, Fort Selden, 23 June 1876.

78. LS, FS, RG 92, NA Captain Barrett to Assistant Adjutant General, Department of Arizona, 31 October 1886.

79. MH, FS, RG 94, M-617, NA, 30 April 1888.

## Chapter 4

1. James Clavell, ed., Sun Tzu, The Art of War, (New York: Delacorte Press, 1983), 47.

2. Don Rickey, Jr., Forty Miles a Day on Beans and Hay: The Enlistedman Fighting the Indian Wars (Norman: University of Oklahoma Press, 1973) 220.

3. Letters Sent, Fort Selden, 1866–1891, Record Group 92, Records of the Quartermaster General, National Archives Microfilm.(LS,FS,RG 92, NA). Microfilm courtesy of the Rio Grande Historical Collections, New Mexico State University. Major Lane to Chief, Quartermaster, District of New Mexico, 12 May 1869.

4. Ibid., 30 May 1869.

5. Ibid., Major Clendenin to Assistant Adjutant General, District of New Mexico, 30 March 1872, 18 May 1872, and 29 May 1872.

6. Medical Histories of Military Posts, 1780–1917, Fort Selden, Record Group 94, Roll M-617, National Archives Microfilm. (MH, FS, RG 94, M-617, NA), Monthly Sanitation Report, 13 February 1875.

7. LS, FS, RG 92, NA, Captain Fetchet to Lieutenant Robinson, 31 October 1989. These ovens, called in Spanish, hornos, are shaped like a large wasps nest.

8. LS, FS, RG 92, NA, Captain Bascom to Chief, Quartermaster, District of New Mexico, 3 July 1882.

9. Ibid., Captain Barrett to Assistant Adjutant General, District of New Mexico, 8 September 1886.

10. Santa Fe New Mexican, 10 September 1872. An extensive search effort was spent trying to find a reference to musquaque, but to no avail.

11. Darlis A. Miller, Soldiers and Settlers: Military Supply in the Southwest, 1861–1885 (University of New Mexico Press, 1989), 173-174.

12. LS, FS, RG 92, NA, Major Clendenin to Assistant Adjutant General, District of New Mexico, 10 March 1873.

13. Ibid., Major Lane to Quartermaster, Fort Selden, 30 June 1869.

14. Mesilla Valley Independent, 23 June 1877. A fanega is a Spanish volume of measure roughly equivalent to 1.58 bushels.

15. LS, FS, RG 92, NA, Post Adjutant to Second Lieutenant D.A. Mitchell, 15th Infantry, 23 August 1881.

16. Ibid., Lieutenant Colonel Devin to the Post Commissary Officer, 21 June 1871.

17. Ibid., Lieutenant Conrad to Assistant Adjutant General, District of New Mexico, 18 October 1875.

18. MH, FS, RG 94, M-617, NA, Monthly Sanitation Report, 24 October 1875.

19. LS, FS, RG 92, NA, Captain MacArthur to Assistant Adjutant General, District of New Mexico, 21 May 1884.

20. Ibid., 29 June 1884.

21. Ibid., Lieutenant Brett to Manager, Nations Meat Market, El Paso, 11 May 1889.

22. Las Cruces Daily News, 5 March 1889. An advertisement in the newspaper showed A.G. Smith to be the proprietor of the City Meat Market.

23. MH, FS, RG 94, M-617, NA, Monthly Sanitation Report, 3 August 1885.

24. Ibid., 31 July 1889.

25. Miller, Soldiers and Settlers, 134.

26. LS, FS, RG 92, NA, Major Clendenin to Chief, Quartermaster, District of New Mexico, 3 June 1870.

27. MH, FS, RG 94, M-617, NA, Monthly Sanitation Report, 27 April 1876.

28. Miller, 149.

29. Santa Fe New Mexican, 28 January 1868.

30. LS, FS, RG 92, NA, Post Adjutant to A.H. Moorehead, 6 October 1874.

31. La Mesilla News, 9 May 1874.

32. MH, FS, RG 94, M-617, NA, Monthly Sanitation Report, 15 August 1885.

33. LS, RG 92, NA, Captain Ellis to Assistant Adjutant General, District of New Mexico, 30 June 1883.

34. MH, FS, RG 94, M-617, NA, Monthly Sanitation Report, 22 June 1875.

35. LS, FS, RG 92, NA, Lieutenant Colonel Devin to Assistant Adjutant General, District of New Mexico, 6 February 1871.

36. Ibid., Major Clendenin to Commanding Officer, Fort Bayard, 11 December 1871.

37. LS, FS, RG 92, NA, Captain Carroll to Commanding Officer, Ft. Craig, 16 December 1876.

38. Ibid., Lieutenant Brett to Commanding Officer, Fort Bayard, 20 September 1889, 17 November 1889.

39. Ibid., Captain MacArthur to Assistant Adjutant General, Department of Arizona, 4 Jan 1886.

40. Ibid., Captain MacArthur to Assistant Adjutant General, Presidio of San Francisco, 15 June 1886.

41. MH, FS, RG 94, M-617, NA, Monthly Sanitation Report, 31 August 1889.

42. Douglas MacArthur, Reminiscences, (New York: McGraw Hill, 1964), 14.

43. Lydia S. Lane, I Married a Soldier: Old Days in the Old Army, (Albuquerque: Horn & Wallace, 1964), 172.

44. MH, FS, RG 94, M-617, NA, Monthly Sanitation Report, 27 April 1876.

45. Ibid., 30 June 1876.

46. LS, RG 92, NA, Major Lane to Assistant Adjutant General, District of New Mexico, 14 May 1869, and 1 June 1869.

47. Ibid., Captain Bascom to Quartermaster, Fort Selden, 1 October 1881.

48. Santa Fe New Mexican, 28 August 1875.

49. Miller, 125-129.

50. LS, FS, RG 92, NA Captain Bascom to Assistant Adjutant General, District of New Mexico, 31 December 1881.

51. Ibid., Captain Tilford to Assistant Adjutant General, District of New Mexico, 29 May 1868. The post had a 12-pound field gun used to fire the morning salute as the flag was raised.

52. Letters Sent, Department of New Mexico, Record Group 393, M-1072, Roll 3, National Archives Microfilm, (LS, DNM, RG 393, M-1072, Roll 3, NA, General Carleton to Major Whitlock, 25 September 1866.

53. LS, FS, RG 92, NA, Lieutenant Colonel Devin to Chief, Quartermaster, District of New Mexico, 1 Jan 1871.

54. Ibid., Lieutenant Colonel Devin to Assistant Adjutant General, District of New Mexico, 1 July 1871.

55. Ibid., Captain Fetchet to Assistant Adjutant General, District of New Mexico, 4 January 1872.

56. Ibid., Lieutenant Colonel Willis to Major Roger Jones, Engineer, St. Louis, 17 June 1866.

57. Ibid., Major Clendenin to Assistant Adjutant General, District of New Mexico, 18 May 1872.

58. Santa Fe New Mexican, 21 July 1868. Blue and black gramma grasses were the best of the local forage grasses in the Mesilla Valley.

59. Miller, 99-102.

60. Santa Fe New Mexican, 21 July 1868.

61. LS, FS, RG 92, NA, Major Clendenin to Assistant Adjutant General, District of New Mexico, 24 December 1873.

62. Ibid., Major Mason to Assistant Adjutant General, District of New Mexico, 28 January 1874.

63. Santa Fe New Mexican, 28 August 1879.

64. Las Cruces Thirty Four, 28 May 1879.

65. LS, FS, RG 92, NA, Capt Bascom to Assistant Adjutant General, District of New Mexico, 19 December 1881.

66. Ibid., Major Clendenin to Assistant Adjutant General, District of New Mexico, 18 October 1870.

67. Ibid.

68. Ibid., Captain Bascom to Assistant Adjutant General, District of New Mexico, 20 April 1882.

69. Ibid., 31 May 1882.

70. Ibid., Major Dubois to Assistant Adjutant General, District of New Mexico, 7 February 1870.

71. Ibid., Lieutenant Colonel Devin to Assistant Adjutant General, District of New Mexico, 11 December 1871.

72. Ibid., Major Clendenin to Assistant Adjutant General, District of New Mexico, 25 October 1872.

73. Ibid., Major Clendenin to Commanding Officer, Fort Craig, 24 December 1873.

74. Ibid., Captain McKibben to Assistant Adjutant General, District of New Mexico, 24 March 1875.

75. Ibid., Lieutenant Cory to Assistant Adjutant General, District of New Mexico, 30 December 1877.

76. Ibid., Captain Haskell to Assistant Adjutant General, District of New Mexico, 3 March 1883.

77. Ibid., Lieutenant Chance to Commanding Officer, Fort Stanton, 10 November 1882. A transit theodolite was used from the highest peak in the Robledo Mountains to Venus to provide a more accurate meridian to assist in map making.

78. Ibid., Captain Carroll to Commanding Officer, Fort Bayard, 11 February 1877.

79. LS, DNM, RG 393, M-1072, Roll 3, NA, Assistant Adjutant General, District of New Mexico, to Commanding Officer, Fort Selden, 10 August 1868.

80. LS, FS, RG 92, NA, Major Clendenin to Assistant Adjutant General, District of New Mexico, 18 February 1873.

81. Ibid., Lieutenant Brett to Commanding Officer, Fort Bayard, 4 June 1889.

82. Santa Fe New Mexican, 25 February 1871.

83. LS, FS, RG 92, NA, Major Clendenin to Assistant Adjutant General, District of New Mexico, 10 June 1872.

84. Las Cruces Borderer, 11 July 1874.

85. LS, FS, RG 92, NA, Lieutenant Corey to Assistant Adjutant General, District of New Mexico, 4 June 1877.

86. Las Cruces Borderer, 11 July1874.

87. LS, FS, RG 92, NA, Captain Bascom to George Davidson, US Coast and Geodectic Survey, 8 October 1882.

88. Letters Received, 1881–1889, Record Group 94, Records of the Adjutant General, Microfilm Series M-689, Roll 91, National Archives Microfilm. Colonel Poe to General Sherman, 17 March 1881.

89. LS, FS, RG 92, NA, Captain MacArthur to Assistant Adjutant General, Division of the Pacific, 15 June 1886

90. Ibid., Captain Ellis to Adjutant General, Department of Missouri, 2 March 1884.

91. Ibid., Captain MacArthur to Mr. White, AT&SF Agent, 17 April 1884.


## Chapter 5

1. Letters Sent, Department (District after 1866) of New Mexico, Record Group 393, Records of the Continental Commands, 1821–1920, Microfilm Series 1072, Roll 3, National Archives Microfilm. (LS, DNM, RG 393, M-1072, Roll 3, NA) General Carleton to the Adjutant General, 9 July 1865.

2. Ibid., General Carleton to Lieutenant Colonel Davis, 5 June 1865.

3. Ibid., General Carleton To Captain Vose, 10 July 1866. Carleton had asked his forts to give up their grain because the Navajos and Apache at Bosque Redondo were starving.

4. Ibid., Major DeForrest to Lieutenant Joseph Bennett, 22 February 1863.

5. Letters Sent, Fort Selden, 1866–1891, Record Group 92, Office of the Quartermaster General, National Archives Microfilm, (LS, FS, RG 92, NA), Captain Brady to Assistant Adjutant General, Department of New Mexico, 14 April 1866.

6. Ibid., Major Osbourne to Assistant Adjutant General, District of New Mexico, 13 July 1874.

7. Ibid., Captain Chance to Commanding Officer, Fort Stanton, New Mexico, 26 September 1862.

8. Santa Fe New Mexican, 7 January 1868.

9. LS, DNM, RG 393, M-1072, Roll 3, NA, General Carleton to Lieutenant Jennings, 24 May 1865.

10. LS, FS, RG 92, NA, Captain Tilford to Assistant Adjutant General, District of New Mexico, 9 December 1867.

11. Ibid., Post Adjutant. to Surgeon, Fort Selden, 4 October 1873, and Captain Carroll to Sheriff, Dona Ana County, 22 November 1876.

12. Ibid.

13. Las Cruces Citizen, 20 August 1953.

14. Medical Histories of Military Posts, Fort Selden, NM, 1780–1891, Record Group 94, Microfilm Series M-617, Records of the Adjutant General, National Archives Microfilm. ( MH, FS, RG 94, NA.) Monthly Sanitation Report, 31 May 1888.

15. LS, FS, RG 92, NA Captain Barrett to Post Surgeon, 15 June 1886.

16. Ibid., Captain Tilford to United States Marshall, Las Cruces, New Mexico 13 July 1868.

17. Ibid., Captain Fechet to Judge Bailey, Las Cruces, 28 March 1870.

18. Ibid., Captain Tilford to Edwin Orr, Las Cruces, New Mexico, 27 January 1867.

19. Ibid., Major Lane to W.L. Rynerson, 16 March 1869.

20. Ibid., Captain Tilford to Judge Lemon, 27 January 1867, and Captain Tilford to Assistant Adjutant General, District of New Mexico, 11 March 1867.

21. Santa Fe New Mexican, 22 June 1865.

22. Ibid., 15 December 1865.

23. Las Cruces Borderer, 30 August 1871.

24. Santa Fe New Mexican, 1 September 1871.

25. Las Cruces Borderer, 30 August 1871

26. LS, FS, RG 92, NA, Lieutenant Colonel Devin to Assistant Adjutant General, District of New Mexico, 30 August and 8 September 1871.

27. Ibid., Lieutenant Colonel Devin to Reynolds and Griggs, La Mesilla, 4 September 1871.

28. LS, DNM, RG 393, M-1072, Roll 3, NA, Headquarters, District of New Mexico to Lieutenant Colonel Devin, 31 September 1871.

29. LS, FS, RG 92, NA, Lieutenant Colonel Duncan to Assistant Adjutant General, District of New Mexico, 12 November 1866.

30. Ibid., Captain Tilford to Assistant Adjutant General, District of New Mexico, 22 February 1868.

31. Ibid., 3 March 1868

32. LS, DNM, RG 393, M-1072, Roll 3, NA, Assistant Adjutant General, District of New Mexico to Commanding Officer, Fort Selden, 9 May 1868.

33. LS, FS, RG 92, NA, Major Clendenin to Assistant Adjutant General, District of New Mexico, 18 June 1870.

34. Timothy Cohrs and Thomas J. Caperton, Fort Selden, New Mexico (Santa Fe: Museum of New Mexico, 1974) 20.

35. LS, FS, RG 92, NA, Captain MacArthur to Superintendent Barr, AT&SF Railroad, 30 January 1885.

36. Ibid., 6 February 1885.

37. Ibid., 23 August 1885.

38. Ibid., Captain MacArthur to Morgan and Company, 8 February 1885.

39. Ibid., Captain MacArthur to Van Patton, 8 February 1885.

40. Ibid., Captain MacArthur to Adjutant General, Department of Missouri, 16 February 1885.

41. Cohrs and Caperton, 22.

42. LS, FS, RG 92, NA, Lieutenant Brett to Adjutant General, Department of Arizona, 12 March 1889.

43. Ibid., Lieutenant Brett to Mesilla Valley Land & Irrigation Company, 31 March 1889.

44. Ibid., Lieutenant Brett to H. H. Llewellyn, 1 June 1889.

45. Ibid., 20 December 1889.

46. Ibid., Lieutenant Brett to Adjutant General, Department of Arizona, 25 December 1889.

47. Ibid., Lieutenant Brett to H. Llewellyn, 3 January 1890.

48. Ibid., Indorsement on Letter to Secretary of the Interior, 13 May 1890. Lea wished to continue to operate the post store after closure for the proposed Indian school.

49. Post Records, Fort Selden 1867–1875, Record Group 94, Records of the Adjutant General, National Archives Microfilm, Courtesy of the staff at the Fort Selden Monument, (PR, FS, RG 94, NA), Court-Martial Records, 3 January 1868.

50. LS, FS, RG 92, NA, Capt Tilford to Mr. Blake, 5 July 1868.

51. PR, FS, RG 94, NA, Court-Martial Records, 9 July 1868.

52. LS, FS, RG 92, NA, Major Lane to Post Trader, 11 March 1869.

53. Ibid., Post Adjutant to Mr Kellner, 8 October 1875.

54. Ibid., 19 October 1876

55. Ibid., Commanding Officer, Fort Selden, to Post Trader, 2 October 1881.

56. Ibid., Captain Barrett to Adolphe Lea, 28 March 1887.

57. Ibid., 8 March 1888.

58. LS, FS, RG 92, NA, Captain Tilford to Assistant Adjutant General, District of New Mexico, 26 March 1868.

59. Ibid., Captain Carroll to Mr. Kellner, 22 October 1876.

60. Ibid., Captain Carroll to General Townsend, Adjutant General, United States Army, 16 December 1876. Morehead became the post trader and there is no further mention of Louis Bailey.

61. MH, FS, RG 94, NA, Monthly Sanitation Report, 21 January 1875.

62. LS, FS, RG 92, NA, Post Adjutant, fort Selden, to E.F. Kellner, 25 September 1875.

63. Las Cruces Citizen, 10 September 1953.

64. Letter from Lieutenant Storey to Miss Annie Cheshire,18 October 1866 courtesy of Fort Selden Staff. Balles is a corrupted form of the Spanish word baile or bailar-to dance.

65. Rio Grande Republican, 5 January 1884.

## Chapter 6

1. Letters Received, Records of the Adjutant General, Records Group 94, M689, National Archives (LR, AG, RG 94, M689, NA) General Sheridan to General Drum, 8 February 1881.

2. Ibid., Colonel Poe to General Sherman, 17 March 1881.

3. Ibid., General Pope to Colonel Williams, 18 January 1882.

4. Chester A. Arthur, Plan for the Construction of Fort Selden, NM: A Message from the President of the United States, (Washington D.C., Government Printing Office, 1882), 428.

5. Rio Grande Republican, 18 June 1881, locals.

6. Fort Bliss is now the largest of the United States military posts in land area.

7. LR, AG, RG 94, M689, Roll 5, NA, General Sherman to the Honorable Robert T. Lincoln, Secretary of War, 30 March 1882.

8. Ibid., Secretary of War, Robert Lincoln to Senator Logan, 30 March 1882.

9. LS, FS, RG 92, NA, Lieutenant Brett to Commanding Officer, Fort Bayard, New Mexico, 20 January 1891.

10. Ibid., Captain MacArthur to Adjutant General, Department of Missouri, 3 November 1885.

11. Ibid., Captain Barrett to Quartermaster General, Washington, D.C., 29 January 1888.

12. Hugh M. Milton II, Fort Selden, Territory of New Mexico, 20.

13. Las Cruces Sun News, 4 August 1972, 3.

# Fort Selden commanders and units 1865–1891

May 1865 to October 1865
    Captain James H. Whitlock
        Troop C, 1st California Cavalry Regiment
        Company F, 1st Mexico Volunteer Infantry Regiment

October 1865 to February 1866
    Captain William Brady
        Troops A and H, 1st New Mexico Volunteer Cavalry Regiment
        Company F, 1st New Mexico Volunteer Infantry Regiment

February 1866 to August 1866
    Lieutenant Colonel E. B. Willis
        Troop H, 1st New Mexico Volunteer Cavalry Regiment
        Company F, 1st Mexico Volunteer Infantry Regiment

August 1866 to November 1866
    Lieutenant Colonel Alexander Duncan
        Troop K, 3rd Cavalry Regiment
        Companies F and I, 125th Infantry Volunteer Regiment (Colored)

November 1866 to December 1866
    Captain Lorenzo Day
        Troop K, 3rd Cavalry Regiment
        Company F, 1st Mexico Volunteer Infantry Regiment

December 1866 to May 1868
    Captain Joseph G. Tilford
        Troop K, 3rd Cavalry Regiment
        Company K, 38th Infantry Regiment

May 1868 to August 1868
    Lieutenant Colonel Curier Grover
        Troop K, 3rd Cavalry Regiment
        Company K, 38th Infantry Regiment

August 1868 to February 1869
    Lieutenant Colonel Edward Bloodgood
        Troop K, 3rd Cavalry Regiment
            Company K, 38th Infantry Regiment

February 1869 to July 1869
    Major William B. Lane
        Troop K, 3rd Cavalry Regiment
            Company K, 38th Infantry Regiment

July 1869 to September 1869
    ` Lieutenant Colonel Edward Bloodgood
        Troop K, 3rd Cavalry Regiment
            Company K, 38th Infantry Regiment

September 1869 to February 1870
    Lieutenant Colonel Frank Stanwood
        Troops H and K, 3rd Cavalry Regiment

February 1870 to March 1870
    First Lieutenant Julian R. Fitch
        Troops H and K, 3rd Cavalry Regiment
        Company E, 15th Infantry Regiment

March 1870 to April 1870
    Captain Edward G. Fechet
        Troops G and I, 8th Cavalry Regiment

April 1870 to May 1870
    Major John M. Williams
        Troops G and I, 8th Cavalry Regiment

May 1870 to December 1870
    Major David R. Clendenin
        Troops G and I, 8th Cavalry Regiment

December 1870 to October 1871
    Lieutenant Colonel Thomas C. Devin
        Troops C and G, 8th Cavalry Regiment

October 1871 to November 1871
    Captain William Kelly
        Troops G and C, 8th Cavalry Regiment

November 1871 to January 1872
    Captain Edmund G. Fechet
        Troops C and G, 8th Cavalry Regiment

January 1872 to June 1873
    Major David R. Clendenin
        Troops G and I, 8th Cavalry Regiment

June 1873 to August 1873
    Captain George W. Chilson
        Troops C and G, 8th Cavalry Regiment

August 1873 to January 1874
    Captain E. W. Whittenmore
        Company F, 15th Infantry Regiment
        Detachment of Troop G, 8th Cavalry Regiment

January 1874 to February 1874
    Major John S. Mason
        Company F, 15th Infantry Regiment
        Detachment of Troop G, 8th Cavalry Regiment

February 1874 to May 1874
    Captain Chambers McKibben
        Company F, 15th Infantry Regiment
        Troop K, 8th Cavalry Regiment

May 1874 to October 1874
    Major N. W. Osbourne
        Company F, 15th Infantry Regiment
        Troop K, 8th Cavalry Regiment (left August 1874)

October 1874 to April 1875
    Captain Chambers McKibben
        Company F, 15th Infantry Regiment
        Detachment of Troop H, 8th Cavalry Regiment

April 1875 to July 1875
    First Lieutenant J. B. Engle
        Company F, 15th Infantry Regiment
        Detachment of Troop H, 8th Cavalry Regiment

July 1875 to March 1876
    First Lieutenant Casper A. Conrad
        Companies G and I, 15th Infantry Regiment

March 1876 to August 1876
    Captain Henry Carroll
        Troop F, 9th Cavalry Regiment
        Company G, 15th Infantry Regiment

August 1876 to October 1876
Captain Charles Hulhammer
Troop F, 9th Cavalry Regiment
Company G, 15th Infantry Regiment

October 1876 to February 1877
Captain Henry Carroll
Troop F, 9th Cavalry Regiment

February 1877 to July 1878
Second Lieutenant William B. Cory
Detachment of the 15'th Infantry Regiment

July 1878 to December 1880 Post Abandoned

December 1880 to May 1881
Captain Louis H. Rucker
Company K, 15th Infantry Regiment
Troop M, 9th Cavalry Regiment

May 1881to June 1881
Second Lieutenant A. R. Paxton
Company K, 15th Infantry Regiment
Detachment from Troop M, 9th Cavalry Regiment

June 1881 to October 1881
First Lieutenant William A. Cory
Company K, 15th Infantry Regiment
Detachment from Troop M, 9th Cavalry Regiment

October 1881 to October 1882
Captain Gustavus M. Bascom
Company B, 13th Infantry Regiment

October 1882 to December 1882
Captain Jesse C. Chance
Company B, 13th Infantry Regiment

December 1882 to April 1883
First Lieutenant Samuel N. Holmes
Company B, 13th Infantry Regiment

April 1883 to May 1883
Captain Joseph G. Haskell
Company B, 13th Infantry Regiment
Detachment from Troop B, 4th Cavalry Regiment

May 1883 to March 1884
   Captain Phillip H. Ellis
      Company D, 13th Infantry Regiment
      Detachment from Troop B, 4th Cavalry Regiment

March 1884 to September 1886
   Captain Arthur MacArthur
      Company K, 13th Infantry Regiment

September 1886 to May 1888
   Captain Gregory Barrett
      Company D, 13th Infantry Regiment

May 1888 to August 1888
   First Lieutenant C. J. T. Clark
      Detachment from Companies A, D, and F, 24th Infantry Regiment

August 1888 to November 1888
   First Lieutenant James E. Brett
      Detachment from Companies A, D, and F, 24th Infantry Regiment

November 1888 to April 1889
   First Lieutenant Henry W. Hovey
      Detachment from Companies A, D, and F, 24th Infantry Regiment

April 1889 to January 1891
   First Lieutenant James E. Brett
      Detachment from Companies A, D, F, and H, 24th Infantry Regiment

22 January 1891 Post Abandoned

Data compiled from Post Returns, Fort Selden, 1865—1891, Record Group 94, Records of the Adjutant General, Microfilm series 617, rolls 1145, 1146, and 1147, National Archives. (Note: The term detachment refers to a group of men smaller than a company or troop)

# Bibliography

## Government Documents

Arthur, Chester A. *Message from the President of the United States, Plan for the Construction of a Military Post at Fort Selden*. Washington, D.C.: Government Printing Office, 1882.

Letters Received, Headquarters, Department of New Mexico, April 1865–September, 1865, Record Group 393 Roll 13, Records of the Continental Commands, Microfilm Series M-1088, National Archives Microfilm.

Letters Received, Headquarters, District of New Mexico, September 1865–January 1891, Record Group 393, Roll 13, Records of the Continental Commands, Microfilm Series M-1088, National Archives Microfilm.

Letters Received, Office of the Adjutant General, 1870–1889, Record Group 94, Roll 142, Microfilm Series M-689, National Archives Microfilm.

Letters Sent, Fort Selden, 1866–1890, Record Group 92, Roll 1, Records of the Quartermaster General, National Archives Microfilm. (These records are now contained in Returns from United States Military Posts.)

Letters Sent, Headquarters, Department of New Mexico, and District of New Mexico, 1849–1890, Record Group 393, Rolls 3 and 4, Records of the Continental Commands, Microfilm Series M-1072, National Archives Microfilm.

Medical Histories of Posts, Monthly Sanitation Reports, Fort Selden, NM, 1871–1891, Record Group 94, Microfilm Series M-617, National Archives Microfilm.

Ninth Census of the United States, Department of the Interior, Population Schedules for New Mexico, Dona Ana County, 1870, Record Group 29, Microfilm Series 583, Roll 893, National Archives Microfilm.

Post Records, Fort Selden 1867–1875, Records of Courts-Martial, Record Group 292, Records of the Continental Commands, National Archives Microfilm.

Returns from United States Military Posts, 1800–1916, Record Group 94, Records of the Adjutant General, Microfilm Series M-617, Rolls 1145-1147, National Archives Microfilm.

*Uniform Code of Military Justice*, Manual for Courts-Martial, United StatesGovernment Printing Office, 1951.


**Newspapers**

*Borderer*. Las Cruces, New Mexico. 1870–1880.
*Citizen*. Las Cruces, New Mexico. 1952–1953.
*Mesilla News*. La Mesilla, New Mexico. 1874.
*Mesilla Valley Independent*. La Mesilla, New Mexico, 1876–1878.
*New Mexican*. Santa Fe, New Mexico. 1863–1891.
*Rio Grande Republican*. Las Cruces, New Mexico. 1870–1884.
*Thirty-Four*. Las Cruces. 1880.
*Weekly Gazette*. Santa Fe, New Mexico. 1867–1870.

# Books

Asburn, P.M. *The Elements of Military Hygiene*. Boston and New York: Houghton Mifflin, 1909.

Clavell, James, editor. Sun Tzu. *The Art of War*. New York: Delacorte Press,1983.

Cleary, Thomas, translator. *Sun Tzu The Art of War*. Boston and London: Shambhala, 1991

Cohrs, Timothy and Thomas J. Caperton. *Fort Selden, New Mexico*. Santa Fe: Museum of New. Mexico Press, 1974, revised 1983.

Craighill, William P. *The 1862 Army Officer's Pocket Companion, a Manual for Staff Officers in the Field*. New York: Nostrand, 1862.

Ferris, Robert G. *Soldier and Brave*. Washington, D.C.: National Park Service, 1971.

Frazer, Robert W. *Forts and Supplies: The Role of the Army in the Economy of the Southwest, 1846–1861*. Albuquerque: University of New Mexico Press, 1983.

—— *Forts of the West: Military Forts and Presidios and posts commonly called Forts West of the Mississippi River to 1898*. Norman: University of Oklahoma Press, 1965.

Heitman, Francis B. *Historical Register and Dictionary of the Army*. Urbana:University of Illinois Press, 1965.

Lane, Lydia S. *I married a Soldier: Old Days in the Old Army*. Albuquerque: Horn & Wallace, 1964.

Lavender, David. *The Southwest*. New York: Harper & Row, 1980

Leckie, William *The Buffalo Soldiers: A Narrative of the Negro Cavalry in the West*. Norman: University of Oklahoma Press, 1967.

MacArthur, Douglas. *Reminiscences*. New York: McGraw Hill, 1964.

Mattes, Merrill J. *Indians, Infants and Infantry: Andrew and Elizabeth Burt on the Frontier*. Lincoln: University of Nebraska Press, 1960.

McKee, James C. *Narrative of the Surrender of a Command of U. S. Forces at Fort Fillmore, NM*. Houston: Stage Coach Press, 1960.

Miller, Darlis A. *Soldiers and Settlers: Military Supply in the South West,1861–1885*. Albuquerque: University of New Mexico Press, 1989.

Miller, Darlis."General James Henry Carleton in New Mexico, 1862–1867." Master's Thesis: New Mexico State University, 1970.

Milton, Hugh M., II. *Fort Selden, Territory of New Mexico*. Las Cruces: Hugh M. Milton II, 1971.

Pearce, T. M. Editor. *New Mexico Place Names: A Geographical Dictionary*. Albuquerque: University of New Mexico Press, 1965.

Prucha, Francis F. *The Sword of the Republic: The United States Army on the Frontier 1783–1846*. Bloomington: Indiana University Press, 1977.

Ricky, Don Jr. *Forty Miles a Day on Beans and Hay: The Enlisted Soldier Fighting the Indian Wars*. Norman: University of Oklahoma Press, 1973.

Thrapp, Dan L. *Victorio and the Mimbres Apache*. Norman: University of Oklahoma Press, 1974.

Utley, Robert M. *Frontier Regulars: The U. S. Army and the Indian, 1866–1891*. Lincoln: University of Nebraska Press, 1973.

## Articles

Billington, Monroe. "Black Soldiers at Fort Selden, New Mexico, 1866–1891." *New Mexico Historical Review*. 62 (January 1967): 65-80.

Cohrs, Timothy. "Fort Selden, New Mexico." *El Palacio* 79 (March 1979): 123-150.

"Fort Selden Ball." *Rio Grande Republican*, 5 January 1884.

Seager, Dorothy. "Amid the Decay of Selden, A Vibrant History Remains." *Las Cruces Citizen*, 4 August 1972.

Stoes, Katherine. "Baseball Game was Big Social Fete." *Las Cruces Citizen*, 10 September 1953.

—— "The Demise of Fort Selden." *Las Cruces Citizen*, 27 August 1953.

—— "The Railroad was 650 Miles Distant when Fort Selden was Built" *Las Cruces Citizen*, 20 August 1953